ESSEX

READY FOR ANYTHING

MICHAEL FOLEY

SUTTON PUBLISHING

First published in the United Kingdom in 2006 by
Sutton Publishing Limited · Phoenix Mill
Thrupp · Stroud · Gloucestershire · GL5 2BU

British Library Cataloguing in Publication Data
A catalogue record for this book is available from the British Library.

ISBN 0-7509-4413-7

To Sarah, Brett, Karen, Tracy and Tina,
for putting up with me as a parent.

Typeset in 10.5/13pt Galliard.
Typesetting and origination by
Sutton Publishing Limited.
Printed and bound in England by
J.H. Haynes & Co. Ltd, Sparkford.

Contents

Acknowledgements

The author would like to express his thanks to the following for permission to use their illustrations: Olive Cooper, the Dagenham Girl Pipers, the Ford Motor Company, Joan Francis, John Smith, Brian Waldon and Sylvia Walker. All other illustrations are from the author's private collection. Although every attempt has been made to find the copyright owners of all the illustrations, anyone whose copyright has been unintentionally breached should contact the author through the publishers.

I would also like to thank the following people for their help in compiling this book: Olive Cooper, Bill Dudley, the East Essex Aviation Museum, Alan Filtness, Joan Francis, Terry Heather, Peter Russell, St Osyth's Local History Society, Ted Slade, John Smith, Jimmy (Les) Underwood, Brian Waldon and Sylvia Walker. Finally, of course, the people of Essex who lived through the Second World War – and especially those who did not.

Introduction

During the Second World War C.A. Jordan, the Director of Welfare for the War Office, made a tour of British troops stationed around the world. He was very impressed with the quality of the canteens and hostels provided for our servicemen. But there was something else that made an impression on him too: it was the look in the eyes of men from Essex when he told them that he had recently been in the county. While people at home were struggling to survive, many of the county's menfolk were doing the same all over the world, but without ever forgetting where they came from.

The Essex that the men serving overseas left was a very different place from the Essex we know today. There were even major developments in the period between the outbreak of war and its end. Some of the changes instigated in public services during the conflict set the standards for society today.

It became obvious when writing this book that Essex during the war was not entirely the quiet, friendly rural place that one suspects it might have been, and that many of the people I spoke to remember it as. Certain beliefs seem to have developed about wartime, such as despite the constant threat of violent death, every person bore the danger with a cheery grin; everyone was pulling in the same direction; and crime did not exist. This may have been true for the majority of the population, but not for everyone. Crime did not stop the day war was declared, but the type of offences committed did change as the conflict went on. New crimes connected with the hostilities appear to have affected the population, and other offences were committed that might surprise some readers. Hooliganism and vandalism may seem like modern problems, but they also occurred during wartime and often involved damage to the most important structures of public safety.

Another aspect of wartime life that became very clear as I spoke to the people who lived through those years was how much effect the First World War was still having on families in 1939. Many of the fathers of those I interviewed were veterans, some with serious wounds, both physical and mental.

One of the strange things that happened in the war, in Essex as well as in the rest of the country, was censorship. The only people who knew where the terror that came from German aircraft and rockets had taken place were those who witnessed the events. It was difficult to balance the need to keep the population aware of the dangers with the desire to prevent widespread panic. Newspapers reported air raids but did not say where the damage occurred. Photographs and cameras were confiscated from many local people, and much of the equipment taken from them was stored in Chelmsford police station. One feature stands out in the photographs that do survive: there is a look about the people – men, women and children, soldiers, civil defence workers and civilians. They all looked ready to face whatever the enemy could throw at them.

ONE

1938: Essex Prepares for War

Although the Second World War did not begin officially until 3 September 1939, much of the 1930s was marred by conflict across the globe. There had been a bitter civil war in Spain and a prolonged dispute between Japan and China. The difference between these wars and previous conflicts was that graphic images of modern bombing and battles were shown on cinema newsreels across Europe. They left little to the imagination as to what was in store for the population of Britain when war with Germany finally came.

It was 1938 when German aims became clear to everyone in Europe, except, it seems, the British Prime Minister, Neville Chamberlain. In February the Germans threatened Austria and the British Foreign Secretary, Anthony Eden, resigned after accusing Chamberlain of appeasing Hitler by taking no action. In March Germany invaded Austria and the following month the country became a German state. Hitler followed his Austrian success by fomenting trouble in the Sudetenland, part of Czechoslovakia. This led to a meeting between Hitler and Chamberlain, and at the end of September 1938 there was a gathering in Munich of the leaders of Germany, Italy, England and France: the Sudetenland was surrendered to Germany. This, however, was never going to be enough for Hitler and eventually he took over the whole of Czechoslovakia.

Although it is always said that Britain was not ready for the coming war, there were some examples of advance preparation. The infrastructure for rationing had been in place since 1936 (although nothing was on ration yet) and there had also been some early organisation of a system of air-raid precautions, in Essex as elsewhere.

Essex in 1938 was not the place that we know today. Many of the county's towns were no more than tiny villages before the war. Many houses had no gas or electricity, and some did not even have running water or a connection to the sewerage system. Heating was by coal fire, the results of which added to the fog that often covered parts of the county.

Although there were vast improvements in the machinery and vehicles being produced for the coming war, on the home front things were not as far advanced. Many farms in the county still relied on horses to do much of the work, such as ploughing. Even school breaks were planned around the rural economy with the

Have
more
ELECTRIC POINTS

and
your
HOME WINS

Many houses in Essex still did not have electricity in 1938. Those that did obviously did not have many electric sockets, hence this pre-war advertisement.

Great Finborough Hall in Suffolk was turned into a Red Cross hospital during the First World War. Joan Francis's mother Edith Watkins, seen here second from the right, was a nurse at the hospital when this photograph was taken on 3 November 1917. She met her husband George Henry, a corporal in the Coldstream Guards, while he was a patient after being gassed in France. *(Joan Francis)*

The wedding of Edith Watkins and George Henry at the parish church, Cockfield, Suffolk, in October 1918. Many couples came together in the First World War and were still suffering its effects, including the lasting results of injuries, when the Second World War broke out. *(Joan Francis)*

Olive Cooper and a friend on Dovercourt beach before it was closed to the public, 1939.
(Olive Cooper)

The beach at Dovercourt before the war. Beacon Hill is visible in the background but as yet it had not been updated with higher Second World War defences.

four main holiday periods being Easter, Christmas, potato-picking and harvest. Farm labourers lived in tied cottages and often had part of their wages paid in wood for the fire.

Joan Francis was a teenager who lived on a smallholding in Thorpe-le-Soken with her mother, two brothers and a sister. Her father had died a few years before as a result of being gassed in the First World War. (It seems that the previous global conflict was still having an effect on the population of Essex even as the next one was about to start.) Joan and her brother were both unemployed. Jobs in the Clacton area were seasonal, mostly connected to the holiday trade during the summer, and Joan remembers that the threat of war made it even more difficult to gain employment, even for her brother who had just completed an apprenticeship.

Olive Cooper lived in Dovercourt and was sixteen in 1939. Living close to the major port of Harwich she witnessed numerous preparations before war was declared. In many areas these included the placing of concrete blocks to stop tanks. The increasing level of activity and preparation made a difference to Dovercourt: despite its proximity to Harwich, changes had always occurred slowly there and it was a very quiet small town. When Olive went back more than fifty years later she still recognised most of the names scratched on the wooden benches on Harwich Pier.

Travel through the county was not as easy in 1938 as it is today. There were no motorways; most of the population did not own a car. Jimmy Underwood lived in Dagenham and remembers that when he was a child it was possible to cross the A13 at any time as there was very little traffic on the road. He also recalls how strict school was in the pre-war period. At Marley Seniors in Dagenham one of the teachers was a Welsh rugby player. He carried a short piece of broom handle which he would use to hit the hand of anyone who spoke. Jimmy left school at thirteen just as the war began.

The railways added to the coal-smoke pollution caused by domestic fires, and the railways were the main form of transport throughout the country. This was how the men who went abroad to fight were carried to their ships. Trains also transported the soldiers who stayed at home but had to move from one camp to another. In addition, they were the means by which most of the raw materials needed for wartime production were moved from their source to centres of manufacturing, and the way finished goods arrived at their final destination.

It would be easy to assume that Essex was an idyllic rural area in 1938 with small villages populated by friendly, caring neighbours. The reality was not quite this ideal. Local newspapers were full of stories about crime. The *Romford Times* seemed to have an endless supply of news reports involving theft and robbery, strange in a time that many remember as a more peaceful and friendly period than today. There were also several examples of gun crime and even an axe attack on a man by his son. The *Romford Times* reported that there was a riot at Hornchurch when a crowd of 400 attacked the Tower Cinema after being told that there were no more tickets available for a concert. Sentencing reflected the international climate when an eighteen-year-old found guilty of breaking into a shop had his punishment deferred to give him the opportunity to join the army.

Pre-war fashion for an Essex girl: Helen Barber from Romford.

A gang of men was arrested in Romford and fined £125 for running football pools. This must have been quite a popular crime among the local population if the number of amateur football teams operating in the area at the time is anything to go by. A more serious offence was recorded when a Brentwood man was arrested on a charge of giving away secrets useful to an enemy. He was tried at the Old Bailey and was reported to have attempted to sell plans of some kind to the Russians. It seems that he had worked for Vickers. He was sentenced to three years in prison. In Dunmow, meanwhile, there was more evidence of gun crime when a solicitor was found dead in an armchair from gunshot wounds. His wife's body was in the garden; she had also died from gunshot wounds.

As early as January 1938 preparations for war were under way. Passengers on trains travelling through Barking were surprised to see bright yellow carriages parked in the sidings. These were mobile Air Raid Precautions instructional units which the railway company was adding to its rolling stock – there were eventually to be seventeen of them. If war broke out, stationmasters were to be responsible for the safety of their passengers and for protecting them from bombing, gas and poison. The new instructional units were to be used to train railway staff to carry out safety operations.

Other preparations were more visible. At the time of the Munich Crisis a gun battery was built on Canvey Island consisting of two 6-inch guns. In fact, planning for war had begun even earlier than this. In 1936 Canvey Island Council wrote to the Air Ministry suggesting that Tewkes Creek would make a suitable seaplane base.

Teams from the Office of Works surveyed large houses all over the county to assess their usefulness as military bases. From 1938 the government had the authority to requisition buildings that were needed for military reasons.

Air-raid precautions were being instigated by March 1938. A display at Maylands Flying Club in Romford by the Air Raid Precaution Squad of the Red Cross and the Women's Air Patrol attracted a large crowd who were no doubt interested in what they might have to face in the future. In Romford there were plans to build dams across the River Rom to provide an emergency water supply for firefighting. There was also a suggestion that the lake in Raphael's Park could be used as another emergency source. The use of local ponds and water systems as supplies for the fire service seems to have been quite common. In Grays the open-air swimming pool was closed so that the water would be available for this purpose.

In Colchester it was decided to recruit and train special constables. This was not a new idea as the town had enlisted a similar force during the General Strike of 1926. The names of the men involved then had been kept on file and they were invited to join the new force; many of them did. In due course they became responsible for patrols to ensure the blackout was being observed, and they were also posted at certain public areas, such as cinemas, the main air-raid shelters and the bus park. The belief was that their presence would make the public feel safer, even if their effectiveness was limited.

In 1939 Southend was still a genteel seaside resort, while the river was the domain of pleasure craft. All of this was soon to change.

Westcliff was still enjoying a summer season in 1938 as the crowds show. The businesses along the front were to close for the duration of the coming conflict.

THE REGULAR ARMY

The Army of to-day offers opportunities which the old soldier never had. Increased pay, better conditions all round and the chance of learning a trade at Government expense. How many jobs in civil life give a pension at about 40 years of age? Even the man who comes out after his 6 or 7 years colour service is practically certain of 9d. to 1s. 3d. a day up to the age of 42 years if he is prepared voluntarily to continue in the Reserve.

No career offers greater facilities for sport of all kinds costing nothing or next to nothing. Many footballers in League Football owe their success to their having learnt to play whilst serving soldiers. There is no sport in the country in which soldiers or ex-soldiers have not made great names for themselves, thanks to instruction and training by experts.

For those whose situation is such as to make active soldiering impossible, there is Supplementary Reserve (Category "C") open to tradesmen and lorry drivers. Service in this entails no training whatever, and annual bounties ranging from £6 to £15 are given according to the trade in which enrolled.

What about it? Information can be had by a written application or personal call at address below or any Army Recruiting Office or Territorial Army Drill Hall.

A pre-war advertisement for the army makes joining up sound a tempting prospect. There is no mention of the coming conflict, however.

Several organisations in the Romford area made requests for volunteers. At a dinner held at the Drill Hall in Romford, the 311th Anti-Aircraft Searchlight Company asked for 500 new recruits. Another 400 were required for the Anti-Aircraft Battalion, Territorials, which already had 40 officers, 1,400 men and drill halls all over Essex. Joining the Territorials was quite an attractive proposition for many men. If a member attended a certain number of drills in a year he could pick up a bounty of around £5 – a welcome amount when some earned less than £1 a week.

In May 1938 a local recruiting office was opened in Chigwell for those wishing to enlist in the Balloon Command. Barrage balloons were to be an important part of defence against enemy air attacks. By August a 70-acre site had opened at Chigwell. It had large hangars for balloons and huts for the airmen, as well as several other buildings to serve the needs of the base. Personnel quickly became involved in local life, especially dances held at the King's Head pub in the town, where they would socialise with nurses from nearby Claybury Hospital.

While recruits were being sought for defence organisations, another vital service was also short of bodies. There was a crisis in recruiting nurses. A health spokesman told the *Romford Times* that nursing was 'a woman's job'. If there was a shortage of applicants then there was either a problem with nursing or a problem with the young girls of the time.

A flying display took place at Hornchurch Aerodrome in May. The Empire Day event attracted around 20,000 visitors and all the proceeds raised went to air force charities.

There were more pleas for volunteer air-raid wardens; male recruits had to be over thirty for obvious reasons but women could be of any age. A building in Romford marketplace was used as a training base for wardens, and uniforms and gas masks arrived within a few months. By September 30,000 gas masks were being stored in a church hall in Gidea Park. The cardboard boxes to hold them were assembled by senior schoolchildren in the town. In the same month Colchester's recreation ground was covered in trenches dug by gangs of labourers. There were more on St John's Green and Holly Tree Meadows. Because of the unexpected lull before war finally came, the trenches became flooded.

The Munich Crisis had an immediate effect on some of the population. Ted Slade was at school in Soho when the events occurred. His school was taken over as an ARP post, which as good as ended his education at the age of twelve. It also led to his father losing his job as a caretaker because the premises he worked at were transferred to the new post. Ted's father then got a job at Briggs Bodies and the family moved to Dagenham. He was paid fortnightly and brought home a white £5 note, the first the family had ever seen. Mr Slade also found the family a house in Whitebarn Lane, Dagenham, for 8s 6d a week. Ted remembers that it had an inside toilet, no bugs and no rats, unlike the one they had come from in Soho.

In Southend an emergency fire brigade was started during the summer and plans were already in place for a complete blackout of the town. Southend had, however,

Romford Market carried on trading throughout the war, although it is doubtful that the number of customers and traders reached anything near the levels of this pre-1939 scene.

been very quick off the mark and had already set up Air Raid Precautions in 1935. Meanwhile, the ARP wardens in Clacton were not having things their own way. They had been used to planning their own working systems and became concerned when the police wanted to direct their working patterns. In Barking the ARP was based at Eastbury House, which was the tallest building in the area at the time, giving the best view of the town. Gas cleaning stations were set up at Eastbury School, the Technical College, Park Hall, Axe Street and at 6 Woodward Road. Early air-raid shelters consisted of covered trenches in strategic sites throughout the borough and sirens were also located in several positions.

Despite the early preparations for air raids, there were many who suspected that planning was inadequate. This view had already been put forward by the mayor of Barking and many people agreed with him. Further defence precautions were not acted upon by the government, however. The Port of London Authority held a meeting to discuss building a barrage across the Thames but the idea was vetoed by Whitehall.

By now the fear of air attack was beginning to have an effect on the population, and different people had different ways of dealing with it. One man accused of stealing a piano accordion from a shop in Romford blamed shell-shock suffered during the First World War and worry about the threatened conflict for his actions. Another man in Dagenham was even more severely affected. His family said that he had also been struck by shell-shock in the previous war and fear of air attacks led to his hanging himself.

That the fear of what was to come was based on fact was shown during a lecture given at Havering village school by a Home Office expert. Thankfully it was for adults, not the school's pupils. The expert went into graphic detail about the effects of gas, which it was believed the Germans would drop during air raids.

The war, when it finally arrived, supposedly brought restrictions, especially to social life and events. However, it is clear that many limitations were in force before hostilities began. There had been several unsuccessful attempts to allow the cinema in Hornchurch to open on a Sunday. Also, a Romford man was fined £2 for allowing his shop to be opened on a Sunday.

Pre-war newspapers are surprisingly full of reports of traffic accidents, especially when one considers the small number of vehicles on the roads then. The high level of accidents and road deaths continued throughout the war. Driving conditions must have been partly to blame for this. The Road Traffic Act of 1930 had abolished the 20mph speed limit and subsequently there was no speed limit at all for vehicles carrying fewer than seven people. Until 1935 there was not even a driving test, and when the test was introduced it only lasted until 1939 and was then suspended until 1946. Roads were less safe in some areas than in others. A coroner's report on an accident black spot at Colchester Road, Harold Wood, reported that although the part of the road controlled by Hornchurch Council was well lit, the Romford section had no lights at all. Not that this made much difference once the blackout started.

In 1930 there were 1 million vehicles on the roads and 7,300 deaths due to traffic accidents. By 1934 there were 1½ million vehicles and 7,000 deaths. Road deaths

Still in use today as offices, this building in Barrack Lane, Harwich, was once the headquarters of the Essex and Suffolk Royal Garrison Artillery which manned the defences at Beacon Hill.

reached 8,272 by 1939 and 9,169 by 1941. Many of these were no doubt due to the introduction of the blackout. There was a report of three blackout-related road deaths in one incident in Dagenham within weeks of the measure's introduction. Indeed, the number of deaths during wartime shows how dangerous road travel was when one considers today's figures of approximately 3,200 deaths a year with 27½ million vehicles on the road.

Despite having the beginnings of civil defence, at the time of the Munich Crisis Britain was still relatively unprepared for war. There were no more than six squadrons of modern reliable fighter planes. The army had been kept quite short of money and resources, and no more than two divisions could have crossed the Channel to fight in Europe at the time. Munich was, however, the turning point. From then on the production of military materiel, including aircraft, increased drastically.

There was an example at this time of how the ties of religion still had a big influence on the population of the county when a Mr Robertson placed an advertisement in the *Essex County Standard* asking for anyone interested in the furtherance of cremation to contact him – the church had always been opposed to cremation. Given what was to happen within a year, it seems Mr Robertson's views made a lot of sense.

Colchester sustained some damage in October in relation not to enemy action but to a very rural event. A bull escaped from the cattle market and ran amok. It attacked a young man riding a bicycle and knocked him to the ground. The animal was finally trapped in Wellesley Road.

Pre-war Essex was not necessarily the caring place that many like to think it. The Bishop of Chelmsford criticised those who complained of the inconvenience that would be caused by taking people evacuated from London if war came. As the bishop pointed out, what was inconvenience compared to being in fear of your life?

As Christmas approached at the end of the last full year of peace there was a heavy snowfall around the east coast of the county. The *Essex County Standard* had a report on seasonal entertainment typical of the time. It said, 'What would Christmas be without a circus?' It also gave its view of what every man in the services would like as a present: home leave.

TWO

1939: The War Begins . . .
or Does It?

In January 1939 Hitler made his feelings clear about the Jewish race in a ranting speech. He stated that a European war would lead to the annihilation of the Jews in Europe. Even the Führer's worst enemy could not have imagined the full horror of what these words would lead to.

Britain, along with the rest of Europe, stood back and allowed Germany to take Czechoslovakia in March. The next objective of the Nazi-led government was Poland, where it tried to reclaim the port of Danzig (Gdansk). Chamberlain had promised support to Poland, so when the country was invaded by Germany in September, Britain could no longer stand back and ignore Hitler's actions. The country was at war.

The declaration of war had an immediate effect. There was a widespread release of prison inmates and boys from borstals. Over 100,000 patients were sent home from hospital, many suffering from serious illnesses, to make way for air-raid victims.

Plans to evacuate the young and weak were already under way. Those with money did not need government aid; it was easy to find a quiet country hotel where the war would not impinge too greatly on their genteel lifestyle.

The population was encouraged to stock up on tinned provisions, jars and dried foods. The adverse effect of this advice was that the better-off could travel from shop to shop buying these items. Ration cards were issued to everyone but the start of rationing was delayed. To help offset the predicted hardship of rationing, a scheme was set in place by the government to encourage everyone to 'Dig for Victory'. Every available piece of open land was turned into allotments to grow vegetables.

When Winston Churchill said that we stood on the abyss of a new dark age, he was talking about the results of a possible Nazi victory. He could just as easily have been referring to the impending blackout. Instructions on the best material to use to prevent light escaping from windows had been given out in July 1939 and the blackout started officially in September.

The end of the month brought the news that income tax was to be raised from 5s 6d to 7s 6d in the pound to help pay for the conflict. The war also reached out to children: the display in Hamley's toy shop window in London was a build-your-own Maginot Line.

❖ ❖ ❖

In 1939 the pace of Essex life went on relatively normally before the declaration of war. In Colchester the site of an old factory was redeveloped into a new public library. However, on its completion in the summer, it was taken over to be used as a food office and fulfilled this role until 1947.

Strange as it now seems given its strong military connections, Colchester was still thought to be safe enough for use as an evacuation reception area for children from London. Other Essex towns were also prepared as reception areas for evacuees. A census was taken in Maldon to locate available accommodation. It found that there were over 12,000 spare rooms in the town. A roll of householders was produced to state how many evacuees each house could take.

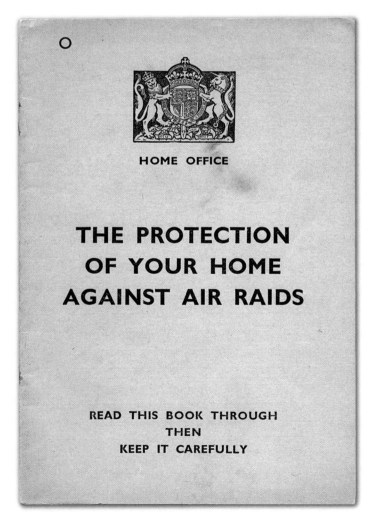

HOME OFFICE

THE PROTECTION OF YOUR HOME AGAINST AIR RAIDS

**READ THIS BOOK THROUGH
THEN
KEEP IT CAREFULLY**

An instruction booklet on what to do if your home was attacked in an air raid. These booklets were given out to householders before war was declared. One can only imagine what effect they must have had on morale.

A letter printed in the air-raid protection booklet explaining how the public needed to play a part in their own defence.

Why this book has been sent to you

If this country were ever at war the target of the enemy's bombers would be the staunchness of the people at home. We all hope and work to prevent war but, while there is risk of it, we cannot afford to neglect the duty of preparing ourselves and the country for such an emergency. This book is being sent out to help each householder to realise what he can do, if the need arises, to make his home and his household more safe against air attack.

The Home Office is working with the local authorities in preparing schemes for the protection of the civil population during an attack. But it is impossible to devise a scheme that will cover everybody unless each home and family play their part in doing what they can for themselves. In this duty to themselves they must count upon the help and advice of those who have undertaken the duty of advice and instruction.

If the emergency comes the country will look for her safety not only to her sailors and soldiers and airmen, but also to the organised courage and foresight of every household. It is for the volunteers in the air raid precautions services to help every household for this purpose, and in sending out this book I ask for their help.

Samuel Hoare

Page 1

At the beginning of the year the Ministry of Health said that no evacuation plans had been made for Romford or Dagenham despite nearby Barking being an evacuation area. Romford and Dagenham were classed as 'neutral areas'. However, it was said that no visitors anxious to escape more dangerous places were to be allowed to move into the area. Brentwood was still unsure of its position – it had not been designated either a neutral or a reception area. Decisions on each town's status were reviewed and adjusted as the war got closer.

*Name of the head of
the household* ....

*Name and address
of your warden* ....

....

....

*Position of nearest
Wardens' post* ....

First aid post ....

Names of members of the household.	Size of respirator [State whether large, medium, small, child's, or infant's.]

Inside the front cover of the air-raid protection book was a section for recording family details.

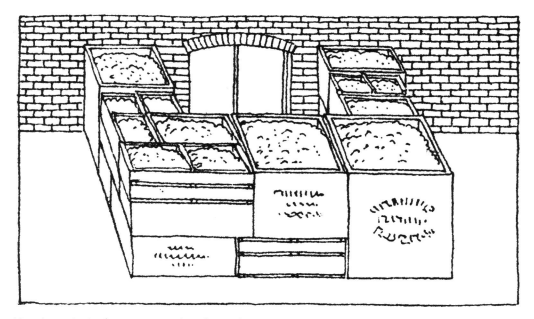

How to protect a basement window from *The Protection of Your Home against Air Raids.*

The expected conflict did bring advantages for some people. Ted Slade had lost his school, which had been turned into an ARP station in Soho. His father had also lost his job as a caretaker, but Mr Slade then got a new job at Briggs Bodies in Dagenham.

Meanwhile, Essex newspapers concentrated on printing reports of normal local life and events. These highlight a significant difference between employment patterns in 1939 and today: the number of men who retired after many years in the same job. The headmaster of Maldon Grammar School retired after twenty-eight years in the post, a printer after sixty years in his job. Obviously sixty-five was not then a recognised retirement age.

Not everyone lasted so long in their employment. Jimmy Underwood left school at thirteen and got a job at Watson's greengrocer's in Broad Street, Dagenham. He was paid 10s a week for six days' work. However, he was soon offeres a better opportunity at the greengrocer's stall on the corner of Heathway and Hedgeman's Road. He was paid 12s 6d for a five-and-a-half-day week. When he told Watson's he was leaving they said they would tell his mum.

The newspapers carried a further piece of work-related news that was a sign of the times. A Mr Fred King from Romford was awarded the MBE for his services to the Post Office. Mr King was the anti-gas instructor for Post Office staff in London.

The violence that was to come from the enemy was not the only danger to the public in 1939. In Barking a man threw a brick at workers in the Labour Exchange. When pursued by a member of staff and Police Constable Tanton he turned and opened fire with a revolver. Neither of the pursuers was hurt and the man was

A cellar or basement is the best position for a refuge-room if it can be made reasonably gas-proof

In a house with only two floors and without a cellar, choose a room on the ground floor so that you have protection overhead

Choosing a refuge room in your home. (*The Protection of Your Home against Air Raids*)

apprehended and placed in Suttons Mental Institution in Hornchurch.

The first Spitfires began to arrive at Hornchurch Aerodrome in February. Over the next few months all the squadrons at the base were supplied with the new planes. This gave the pilots ample time to get used to them before the war began.

Romford Council had applied to be one of the first boroughs to get Anderson shelters. The councillors were not happy about the amount of money allocated to pay for the shelters but they still received 450 of them in February. At Tilbury 900 Anderson shelters were delivered in April. They were supposed to be sunk into the ground but the marshy soil of the riverside town presented problems and the structures flooded. This was also common in other parts of Essex that bordered the River Thames. Although the Anderson shelters were extremely effective against anything short of a direct hit, they had one big drawback: they were made to go in the garden and only a quarter of the population had a garden.

The Women's Voluntary Service (WVS) in Colchester was greatly expanded in April. Although it had been formed the previous year, initially the organisation was run on a small scale. Members now began a survey of available accommodation in preparation for the expected arrival of evacuees. They also took part in salvage collections, knitted for the forces and undertook numerous other activities throughout the war period. Despite its later expansion, the WVS was always an essentially middle-class association. It was made up of the type of women who would organise village fêtes in peacetime, the kind of activity that working-class women did not have time for.

In May the government decided that there would be no conscription for those

Another government booklet for the public. It listed the types of National Service available to assist the war effort.

APPLICATION FOR ENROLMENT

This application should be completed and detached, folded as directed overleaf, and posted to or left at the appropriate address as shown in the Guide. (If posted no stamp is required.)

SECTION I — *For use by Applicant.*

(1) Surname ....

(IN BLOCK LETTERS and stating whether Mr., Mrs. or Miss)

(2) Christian names ....

(3) Age ....

(4) Full home address ....

....

....

(5) Service which it is desired to enter ....

....

....

(6) Present occupation ....

(7) Usual occupation if different from that shown in item (6)

....

(8) If employed, state Employer's name and address (if own employer, state " on own account ").

....

....

(9) Employer's business ....

Signature of applicant ....

SECTION II — *For official use by the Ministry of Labour.*

Occupational sub-Classification No. ....

Decision as regards Occupation:
(a) Applicant may be enrolled.
(b) Applicant may be enrolled only in the capacity of

....

(c) Applicant may not be enrolled.

Signature of M/L Officer ....

Date ....

FURTHER COPIES OF THIS FORM CAN BE OBTAINED AT ANY POST OFFICE OR LOCAL OFFICE OF THE MINISTRY OF LABOUR.

The application form for enlisting for National Service. *(National Service)*

serving in the Territorials. This led to a rush of recruits at Territorial drill halls across the county. The following month conscription registration was started for twenty and 21-year-olds.

June saw the first serious blackout practice in Colchester. The RAF was enlisted to help test the effectiveness of the trial and it worked very well. The drill must have given the population of the town some idea of what to expect when war came.

Army bases in the county were making preparations well before the outbreak of hostilities in September. In July hundreds of militiamen arrived at Shoebury Barracks for training. One of the recruits of what was eventually to become 22 Medium and Heavy Training Regiment was Gunner Frankie Howerd. Despite being well below standard in military terms, he went on to achieve fame in his chosen career as a comedian. It was while at Shoebury that he began to display his talent, appearing in entertainment events put on for the other men.

Although war was still not officially declared, the first of the many pilots from Hornchurch to give their lives died in August. The Spitfire flown by young Cyril Gower, who had just arrived at the base, suffered engine failure. He managed to steer it away from houses before crashing on the playing field at what is now Grays School. He died in the crash. At about this time the married quarters at Hornchurch

Ebenlowelle Walker was a young family man from Dagenham. With thousands of others he became a soldier and ended up in parts of the world he had never dreamed of seeing. *(Sylvia Walker)*

airbase were evacuated of women and children to make way for the increased number of men who would be serving there.

The Essex Public Assistance Committee decided to raise the scales of relief in the county. There were high levels of unemployment throughout the thirties and even the expected war did not entirely eradicate this social problem. To meet the increased cost of living, rates were raised by a shilling for adults and sixpence for children. The miserly increase can have done little to combat poverty among the underprivileged, even though prices were lower than today. There was a further example of the hardship suffered by some when many casual wards (part of the workhouse system) were closed to tramps. One gentleman of the road took drastic action in Braintree when he was refused entry to the local casual ward. He threw a stone through the window of the Freeman, Hardy & Willis shop. When arrested he admitted doing it on purpose so that he would be locked up and bring the outrage to the attention of the public.

In August covered trenches were dug in public parks in Romford and surrounding areas. These were not for use as general shelters but were for anyone caught out by an unexpected raid. The borough council told journalists that the population was calm and was prepared to meet whatever was to come with fortitude. However, the same page of the *Romford Times* carried the story that a large group of mothers had just marched on Hornchurch council offices demanding adequate protection from air raids.

Rumours of all kinds were rife in the war years, but one that started before hostilities even began was that the Dagenham Girl Pipers were disbanding. The pipers were formed by the Revd. J.W. Graves in the newly built town of Dagenham in the 1920s. In what may seem a strange move, he brought together a group of girls from a town on the edge of East London in a pipe band more suited to the culture of Scotland. But the idea worked and the Dagenham Girl Pipers became famous all over the world. When war broke out one group of girls from Dagenham was touring Germany. When this trip was cancelled, and some of the girls went off to do war work, the newspapers printed stories reporting that the pipers had been

Gertrude Walker was bringing up her four children with her husband in Dagenham when the war broke out. When her husband went off to fight, her two older children were evacuated with their school while Gertrude, Peter (seen in the photograph) and Sylvia were evacuated together. *(Sylvia Walker)*

There were rumours that the Dagenham Girl Pipers had disbanded because of hostilities, but this booklet shows how they played their part in the war effort all over the world. *(Dagenham Girl Pipers)*

disbanded. It caused uproar throughout the country. The truth was that the band carried on through the war years, entertaining the troops and others. Some full-time band members were joined for evening performances by part-timers who did war work all day.

Evacuation began before war was even declared and children were sent to supposedly safer parts of the country. They began to leave at the end of August and usually travelled as a group with their school. Most evacuees were transported by train, but there were some exceptions. Children from Hunters Hall School in Dagenham were taken in open-topped lorries to Tilbury Docks where they were loaded aboard a ship and taken to Great Yarmouth. Some of them remember seeing the periscope of a submarine that travelled alongside as an escort. Other Dagenham children boarded ships at Dagenham Dock. Some from Tilbury were evacuated by river. Many of the pleasure steamers that had plied their trade among day-trippers on the Thames were used to carry evacuees to other parts of the country. Other

A small child's gas mask and carrying box. The string was used to carry the box on the shoulder.

Conditions for possession of a gas mask. This message was printed on the outside of the box.

THIS SPECIAL RESPIRATOR FOR A SMALL CHILD IS GOVERNMENT PROPERTY. ANY PERSON WHO HAS IT IN HIS POSSESION IS RESPONSIBLE IN LAW FOR USING CARE TO KEEP IT IN GOOD CONDITION. IT IS TO BE RETURNED TO THE LOCAL AUTHORITY IN WHOSE AREA THE POSSESSOR MAY BE AT ANY TIME, EITHER ON REQUEST OR WHEN NO LONGER REQUIRED

children did not go too far outside London. Brentwood, for example, was used as a reception area. Householders in the town were paid 10s 6d a week for each child they took into their home.

Many feared that the arrival of children from the slums of London would be a great culture shock to both the family receiving them and the evacuees themselves. That was not the case in Maldon where most of the evacuees came from Woodford and Wanstead, which, although close to London, were at the time still quite rural. In fact, the only difference between the evacuation and reception towns was that Maldon was closer to the sea. Most evacuees arriving in Maldon were from middle-class families. (Like other reception areas in Essex, such as Colchester, Maldon later became an evacuation area itself as the threat of invasion grew.) Other areas were not as lucky with their evacuees and some parts of Essex found themselves forced to deal with children who had come from inner-city London and who had little or no knowledge of the countryside. Often the children had little experience of cleanliness either. This frequently meant that bed-wetting was a nightly occurrence and led to endless washing, a significant chore in the days before washing machines.

Many children arrived with only the clothes they were dressed in. This prompted a rush to buy clothes in the reception town, which would often exhaust the whole available supply. There were reports that in some areas residents with the largest houses received fewest evacuees.

PACKAGING OF RESPIRATOR

1. The respirator should be placed in box with heavy end (container) standing on bottom of box.

2. Care must be taken to see that the expiratory outlet valve lies flat against the side of the box without deformation.

WHEN RESPIRATOR IS REQUIRED FOR USE

1. Hold respirator by the harness.
2. Put on by first putting chin into face-piece and then draw harness over head. Join free parts of harness by hook and eye provided.
3. Take off by pulling the harness over head from the back.

DO NOT TAKE RESPIRATOR OFF BY PULLING THE CONTAINER UPWARDS OVER THE FACE.

Instructions for use of a gas mask. These were printed inside the lid.

Some believed that the people organising billeting were sympathetic to those who moved in similar social circles.

Terry Heather was eight when the war began. He remembers his parents receiving a letter before the war started asking if they would allow him to be evacuated. They agreed and he became one of group who assembled at Dorothy Barley School, Dagenham, carrying a gas mask. Several children also carried a small suitcase or a carrier bag. Four double-decker buses took them to a local underground station from where they were transferred to a main-line station. They were taken to Langport in Somerset. Although he remembers little about the journey, one thing stood out in his mind: at the end of the railway carriage was a man playing 'Wish me luck as you wave me goodbye' on an accordion.

Upon arrival the children were taken into a hall full of adults. There was a stage with a large table, which was full of biscuits, corned beef and other items. As the children were placed with a family they were given provisions from the table to take with them. Terry went to the home of a policeman, along with two other children who were brother and sister. Three children were too much for the family, however, and it was Terry who eventually had to leave. He was placed in four different homes during his time in Somerset.

By now cinema newsreels were showing refugees fleeing the Nazis in Europe and the children being evacuated must have seen themselves as being in a similar situation. Schools were among the resources which were overstretched in reception areas. In many cases the problem was overcome by the introduction of part-time schooling – morning classes for local children and afternoon classes for evacuees.

Sylvia Walker lived in Dagenham, in Martin's Gardens. She was one of five children. Her three older siblings were evacuated to Devon with their schools while Sylvia and her younger brother were taken to Swindon by their mother who stayed with them. Sylvia had little idea about what was going on at home – she was six at the time and did not really care, because she was very happy with the Swindon family. Her mother must have been receiving letters from her father who was serving in Egypt as she often mentioned him. Sylvia remembers the war years as much happier times than today. Although the family had few possessions, they were content, the neighbours were friendly and they could leave the key hanging on a string inside the front door without worrying. She also remembers having great respect for teachers, respect reinforced by the threat of the cane. There was little cheek given to teachers in those days.

The residents of some Essex towns were surprised to receive evacuees when their own area seemed to be in so much danger. North Weald was the site of an RAF airfield and yet was still a reception area early in the war. Later, along with other Essex reception areas, it became an evacuation area and children left, which meant that the schools shut down. Some of the teachers who remained set up home-teaching schemes so that groups of children who had also stayed behind could be taught in their parents' homes on a part-time basis.

There was a strange discrepancy in the allowances paid for children. An evacuated child was allowed the 10s 6d a week allowance, and yet the offspring of men serving as privates in the forces were only allocated 5*s* for the first child, 3*s* for the second and 2*s* for the third.

Another preparation for the coming conflict was the inspection of all hospitals, among them the County Hospital in Colchester. It was rated as a first-class infirmary that could take all types of cases and was enlarged to 269 beds. Nevertheless, resources were stretched by a polio epidemic in the months just before the declaration of war.

Several changes had to be made to the hospital to take account of the different needs of the population in the event of hostilities. Air-raid shelters were built and plans were drawn up for the establishment of an emergency hospital if the building was damaged beyond use. Over 1,000 blood donors were recruited and a mobile resuscitation team was formed to go out to air-raid sites. Among the new regulations governing hospitals was the requirement that ninety beds be kept empty for emergencies.

In August an anti-aircraft battery was set up at Bowater's Farm close to Coalhouse Fort. This was a sandbagged position with mobile guns manned by the Territorial Army. It was one of many such positions set up along the Thames using whatever weapons were available. Like other defences, the Bowater's Farm battery developed over the war period as more efficient guns became available.

The airport and the pier at Southend were both requisitioned in August, although the public were still allowed access to the pier until early September. The train that ran to the end of the pier was responsible for carrying over a million servicemen in the course of the war. These were the fit and able-bodied on their way to troopships moored at the pier's end and wounded being brought ashore. All shipping entering and leaving the Thames during the war was controlled from the pier or from Royal Terrace, which had also been taken over by the navy.

When war was finally declared in September many of those who had previously been volunteers, such as the ARP wardens, began to be paid, not that they had much to do for some time after the declaration of hostilities.

There was a mixed reaction to the outbreak of war when it came. For some it was an event that had been expected for so long that the declaration was merely the final confirmation. For others it was a terrifying occasion that was to change their lives. Whatever an individual's personal feelings, everyone who witnessed it remembers what he or she was doing that day.

Joan Francis clearly recalls the day war was declared. She was nineteen by then and with two friends she went to Clacton beach. The weather was beautiful but the people on the beach were not sunbathing; they were filling sandbags. Joan also recollects being given a gas mask, which she ignored because there were no signs of the war in Essex at the time.

John Smith was seventeen when war was declared. He lived in Romford with his parents, two brothers and a sister. He remembers Romford as a quiet market town where everyone was friendly and there was no bother from yobs or undesirables. He worked at S.W. Adams, ironmonger and builders' merchants, in the marketplace. He had started there at fourteen as a shop boy on 10*s* a week. In the months leading up to the war John recalls feeling worried about the inevitability of conflict. However,

Joan Francis on the family smallholding, The Elms in Thorpe-le-Soken. *(Joan Francis)*

along with others who were young at the time, he also recalls a feeling of excitement.

There had been a brief period when it was hoped that war would not come. The relief that people felt when Chamberlain came back from Germany on 30 September 1938 waving his piece of paper was, however, short-lived. John Smith's father had been badly wounded in the trenches during the First World War and believed that another conflict was inevitable. Like other First World War veterans he spoke little about his experiences. Terry Heather from Dagenham never knew that his father had been a POW in the first war until he died and a letter from the king was found in his belongings welcoming him home from captivity.

As well as working for Adams, John Smith joined the ARP as a messenger boy when war became imminent. Two days after the declaration he found himself manning the switchboard at Romford Town Hall, alone. His instructions were to contact several local dignitaries if a 'yellow' or a 'red' call came through. He says he doubts the people of Romford would have slept so soundly that night if they knew that their safety was the responsibility of a seventeen-year-old boy.

Rumours were widespread about what would happen in the coming days and months. Many believed that there would be no direct evidence of the war in Britain and that Germany would simply be blockaded by the Royal Navy. There were even rumours of secret weapons that used rays to find enemy aircraft and to cause their engines to cut out, which would stop any bombing.

Many people left some coastal areas of Essex and travelled further inland away from what they obviously thought was going to be an early invasion. As the population in East London dropped, the number of people in East Anglia rose and the increase seems to have been in the areas away from the coast. The shift in population became clear when the government later banned the award of any further war contracts to companies in Chelmsford. This was due to the serious overcrowding in the town.

Joan's family at The Elms, Thorpe-le-Soken, a few years before the war. From left to right: Edith, Dulcie, Joan and Norman. Joan's mother ran the smallholding because her husband George was an invalid after being gassed in the First World War. Not many veterans received pensions, even the wounded ones, so times were hard. *(Joan Francis)*

The effects of war on Essex coastal towns were catastrophic: not only did a proportion of the population move away, the holiday industry died overnight, leaving many workers unemployed. Lists of areas that could no longer be visited were posted at London railway stations and these included most of the towns on the county's coast. In Clacton the effect on the recently opened Butlin's Holiday Camp was immediate. Billy Butlin had been in the town the weekend war was declared, trying to reassure his customers, but the government instantly took over the camps for war use. Butlin's at Clacton became an internment camp.

At the time, Billy Butlin was running a successful business that built camps at £75 per hut. The government was paying £150 for each of its huts, so Butlin was given the job of constructing camps for the government for the use of troops, workers, internees and prisoners. Part of the deal was that he could buy back his own camps after the war for three-fifths of the price the government had paid for them.

By now the railway had come under government control. Under the Emergency Powers Act it was running both London Transport and the main-line railways. It was this central control during wartime that was the catalyst for nationalisation of the network after the war.

In September 1939 some parts of the east coast were already fortified. Harwich still had the Beacon Hill Battery, which had been in use in the First World War, with its two 6-inch guns, but most of the harbour's firepower was concentrated on the Suffolk side of the river. Because the manning of coastal defence guns was a Territorial Army function, the Royal Engineers and Royal Artillery units involved

The seaside town of Clacton and its entertainments for visitors. Soon there would be a change in the nature of the structures that dominated the area as defences were built to deter visitors, especially those coming from the sea.

Call to National Service
FROM THE PRIME MINISTER

10, Downing Street,
Whitehall,

January, 1939.

The desire of all of us is to live at peace with our neighbours. But to ensure peace we must be strong. The Country needs your service and you are anxious to play your part. This Guide will point the way. I ask you to read it carefully and to decide how you can best help.

Neville Chamberlain.

A letter from Prime Minister Neville Chamberlain explaining how it was the desire of everyone to live in peace. Strange, then, that the letter was printed in the *National Service* booklet given out to the population to explain how they could help in the event of a war. *(National Service)*

were raised in coastal areas. The guns at Harwich were manned by the Suffolk Heavy Regiment, Royal Artillery (TA), while the searchlights were manned by the Fortress Company, Royal Engineers (TA). While other searchlights were used to pinpoint aircraft, those on the coastal defences were also used to find enemy shipping. Many of the soldiers based at these sites were young men under the age at which they could be sent overseas. There was, of course, constant change in personnel as they reached the required age and were posted to other units.

Olive Cooper lived in Dovercourt with her parents. She remembers there being plenty of room for the newly arrived soldiers – there were lots of empty houses in the town because so many people had left. Her father and brother were in the navy, as might be expected in a sea-going area. She recalls barrage balloons being raised along the coast. The family built an air-raid shelter in the back garden. The younger children were evacuated from the town to somewhere in the West Country but Olive, who was sixteen, stayed at home. She worked in the local Co-op and found there were no problems when rationing began. The customers accepted the situation and made the best of what was available to buy. A Warner's Holiday Camp had opened in the town just before the war and although it was closed to holidaymakers, it became a home for Jewish refugees.

Following Chamberlain's declaration, the war in the air took an early tragic turn on 6 September with the Battle of Barking Creek. It was the first time that Spitfires from nearby Hornchurch had fired their guns in anger. Unfortunately, a mistake by a radar station meant the 'enemy' turned out to be a flight of Hurricanes from North Weald. Two of the Hurricanes were shot down and, at the age of nineteen, M.L. Hulton-Harrop became the first British pilot to die in the war.

Civilians from Essex were caught up in hostilities almost immediately. An Upminster family was aboard the *Athena*, which was torpedoed three days after war was declared. The Milbourne family – a couple and their two children aged nine and four – had been on their way to Canada. Thankfully they were later reported to be safe.

Security in the county was quickly stepped up after 3 September. A woman of German origin was fined £6 at Chelmsford for failing to register as an alien. Even more interesting is the fact that she was also charged with carrying a camera without permission. Another new wartime law banned dogs from being out at night. It was introduced after an air-raid warden was attacked and bitten while on duty.

Following the initial panic at the outbreak of war things quickly settled down into a more normal routine. In Romford by 13 September the cinemas had reopened and greyhound racing was taking place again at the town's dog track.

November saw one of the first naval casualties of the war off the Essex coast. German planes were seen dropping something off Harwich. This was months before air raids began in any other part of the country. Amid uncertainty about what these weapons were, the anti-aircraft guns were ordered to stop firing. Ships were then sent out to investigate and unfortunately were all too successful in finding the dropped items, which turned out to be magnetic mines. HMS *Gypsy* was struck and sank with many casualties within sight of the shore. Olive Cooper remembers hearing the loud bang as the *Gypsy* hit the mine. The blast shook the whole town.

TO BLACKOUT RIDERS

YES—SHE **DID SEE** YOU COMING, BUT . . .

she didn't realize that you couldn't see her — that was the trouble. You *must* ride so that at any moment you can pull up within the range of your vision.

RIDE **S-L-O-W-L-Y**

IN THE
BLACKOUT

Issued by the Ministry of War Transport

The advantages of the blackout did not always outweigh the problems it caused as this government advertisement shows.

Although bombing on the mainland did not begin until much later, from early in the war the Thames was the site of constant raids by the Germans, who mainly dropped magnetic mines into the river in an attempt to destroy shipping. Because of this, a branch of the Portsmouth mine school, HMS *Vernon*, was opened at Brightlingsea. Its men were responsible for destroying the mines.

Harwich experienced the effects of the war before much of the rest of the country. The Royal Navy took over the Great Eastern Hotel as its headquarters. Several Polish ships had escaped the invasion of their country and were moored in Harwich Harbour.

During the early days of the conflict, vessels from the town were still taking soldiers across to France. The train ferries carried heavy equipment to the continent, including tanks and lorries, most of which were later abandoned on the beaches at Dunkirk.

Although rationing had not yet started, the system was already in place and the idea of being careful with food was promoted by everyone. The *War Pictorial Magazine* offered a prize of 5*s* for the best economical wartime recipe. This was printed as early as September, within weeks of the beginning of the war.

The way of life for the civilian population changed dramatically despite the lack of enemy action. The cinemas showed newsreels of the Russian–Finnish War, and after the film audiences exited into streets that were as dark as the picture-house they had just left. The blackout caused at least as many problems for the home population as it did for the enemy. Infringements of blackout regulations led to fines and therefore meant that over a million previously innocent people ended up with a criminal record. In addition, during air raids it was difficult to light Anderson shelters. The recommended covering for shelter doorways was sacking soaked in water to stop gas. This was not good blackout material, however. The blackout material in most homes consisted of thick, dark cloth or paper on batons which was then fitted to windows. The cloth, at 2s a yard, soon ran out. This led to the need to improvise by painting thinner material with powdered lampblack mixed with water. It was not a pleasant alternative as it had a strong aroma.

At Hornchurch Aerodrome security was not a high priority at the beginning of the war. The airmen at the site had a hand in guarding the field and were issued with rifles. One guard panicked at a sudden noise one evening and fired his gun. The next day he found that he had shot a cow.

The war was not the only hardship the population of Essex had to bear. The winter of 1939/40 was the harshest to date in the twentieth century. The cold weather did have one advantage, however, in that to some extent it restricted enemy action, although for the first few months German forces were too busy elsewhere to concentrate firepower on Britain.

There were several false alarms in the early days of the war. For many people these were a novelty rather than a reason to panic. Instead of rushing off to shelters, many went outside to look up into the sky to see who was coming to bomb them. Schools were open in many areas but only if they had air-raid shelters.

This summer storm did not deter the crowds at Clacton in the summer of 1939. A different kind of storm kept them away for a number of years after this picture was taken.

The cliffs at Holland-on-Sea were still undeveloped in the pre-war years but they quickly became the site of pillboxes and other defences as the threat of invasion loomed.

There was an early example of restrictions on the media in November when a press day was held at Shoebury Ranges. Reporters from most national newspapers attended and as one journalist wrote, 'I am not allowed to tell you where I am but as it is the only place of its kind in England that seems absurd.' While the press were present two magnetic mines were dropped in the Thames and were dealt with by bomb disposal men. The reporters were not allowed to tell anyone about this until the following March. Indeed, there were many restrictions on reporting events during the war. Often disasters were mentioned without naming the location of the event, and there was usually a 28-day ban on publishing information about bomb damage. Lack of detail in the newspapers could, however, lead to the spread of rumours.

There were some positive developments in Essex early in the war. The County Council came up with a scheme to top up the pay of married employees who were serving in the forces, a welcome bonus to those surviving on low army wages. There was also relaxation of some outdated restrictions. A law was passed by Parliament and stated that on receipt of a certificate from the relevant military authority, local councils were to be allowed to open cinemas on a Sunday for the entertainment of the troops.

There were further signs of the conflict when a mine in the North Sea sank the Dutch liner *Simon Bolivar* in November. Seventeen survivors were taken to the

County Hospital in Colchester. They were so thickly covered in oil that the hospital staff thought they were all black. They also believed one of them was a girl and only discovered that he was male the next morning after he had spent the night in a women's ward.

The war had an early effect in Southend. Gun emplacements were erected at Belfairs and at Thorpe Bay, and the pier was attacked by German aircraft in the same raid in which the two mines were dropped at Shoebury.

Like hospitals, supplies of medicines and drugs now had to be safeguarded. At the May & Baker chemical factory in Dagenham the danger of attack was taken into account as soon as war was declared. As a result stocks of important drugs were taken from the factory and stored in several safer places around the country, including a railway siding in Wales. The absence of the expected early bombing gave the authorities a chance to fortify the factory. Part of the defences involved direct telephone contact with nearby Hornchurch Airfield and the buildings were even painted in camouflage colours. Unfortunately, it was impossible to disguise the railway lines that ran alongside.

Not all defences were built specifically for the war – some older structures were reused. One of these sites was Tilbury Fort, whose origins lie in a blockhouse built by Henry VIII. The fort became the site of the Gun Operations Room which

Beacon Hill at Harwich with the high watchtower that was built as part of the Second World War defences. In previous conflicts the defences had been lower so as to be more difficult to hit in an attack from the sea.

controlled the anti-aircraft defences of the Thames and the Medway. The control room was set up in the fort's chapel. This moved to a newly built site at Vange in 1940. An even older site put to war use was Colchester Castle's vault. When the air-raid sirens sounded, a few of the less intrepid locals would go down to the vault for safety.

Other military sites were adapted from their original use. Shoebury Garrison, which had been mainly occupied by the men who guarded the artillery-testing site there, became a transit camp for other soldiers. Huts were erected on the cricket field in much the same way as during the First World War. The camp gymnasium was also used to house troops. Others were billeted in private homes around the town. Many of these men were from the 5th Maritime Regiment which provided artillery protection for merchant shipping entering and leaving the Thames Estuary.

A boom was built part of the way across the river at Shoebury and a similar construction was erected on the Kent side, leaving a narrow gap for shipping to pass into the Thames. This gap was closed with a submarine net to deny U-boats access to the river. Along with other beaches in the county, those at Shoebury were mined and lined with coiled barbed wire. The wire had two functions: it would make it difficult for any invading force to move inland from the beach and it kept local people away from the minefields.

The end of the year saw no move closer to a real war for most of the country. Essex had been as badly affected by enemy action as any other county, but the disruption and destruction was at a much lower level than had been expected.

The most lethal weapon working against Britain was self-imposed – the blackout. Road deaths increased in 1939, and these figures do not take into account those who died in a fall in the darkness. The most lethal threat was trolley buses because they ran so silently on their tracks. An added danger in the blackout was thick fog which was made even more dense by the smoke from coal fires.

The blackout also had a devastating effect on social life. A popular pastime in pre-war town centres was window-shopping. It was normal to see many people looking in brightly lit shop windows in the evening, especially after the cinemas turned out. This activity came to an abrupt end when the shop lights were turned off.

Travel meant sitting in dimly lit railway carriages with blacked-out windows and then getting out at dark stations where the place-name signs had been removed. Anyone who fell asleep on a train could have serious difficulties finding out where they were when they woke. The best thing to do was to stay at home in the evenings behind the thick black curtains that hid the light and listen to the single radio station, the Home Service.

Even Christmas was a tame affair for most. At Hornchurch the only enter-tainment for airmen and locals was the Station Cinema, and that only showed films at the weekend. One bright spot appeared on the local airfield that Christmas when the Windmill Girls came down from London to give a show.

THREE

1940: Now It's for Real

The Phoney War continued for a number of months into 1940. By January many of the children who had been evacuated had returned home again. However, the fall of France in June led to new fears of an invasion. Indeed, Hitler had formed an invasion plan called Operation Sealion, but the Führer knew that he had to gain supremacy in the skies before it could be put into practice. In a speech he stated that the Luftwaffe would overcome the RAF with all means at its disposal as quickly as possible. So began the Battle of Britain.

The German Army was not yet ready to launch an assault on Britain anyway. It was occupied elsewhere, invading Denmark and Norway in April. In the same month the Nazis constructed Auschwitz. In May, after receiving severe criticism over the Norway campaign in which British troops were forced to withdraw, Chamberlain resigned and Churchill became Prime Minister. Germany, meanwhile, invaded Holland, Belgium and Luxembourg. In the same month German nationals, including Jews who had fled the Nazis, were interned in Britain.

From the British point of view, this was the year the country had to make every effort to rearm after leaving the majority of its military equipment on the beaches of Dunkirk. It was also the year when people came forward in their thousands as Local Defence Volunteers to help protect their country, often armed with no more than a knife tied to a broomstick.

A new Minister of Food appointed in 1940, Frederick James Marquis, 1st Earl of Woolton, was responsible for persuading the population that there were benefits to rationing, which finally began in January. Rationing was actually a much fairer system than the free-for-all that had operated before. However, it was not only the public who had to deal with shortages; shopkeepers had to cope with restrictions and numerous rules, too, while still running their businesses.

Germany's ally Italy became involved in the war by invading Egypt from Libya in September. The following month the Italians invaded Greece. In October, too, the main focus of the war at sea shifted to the Atlantic where U-boats were inflicting horrendous losses on Allied vessels. Over 400,000 tons of shipping were destroyed in October alone.

❖ ❖ ❖

The effect of rationing was felt most acutely by women who had to face big queues for goods. They often did this after a long day spent in important war work in factories or as drivers. There was also the problem of what to cook when they finally got home with their purchases: there were no convenience foods then and in some households it was necessary to light a fire to get hot water or to cook. Not everyone had a gas stove. To add to the difficulties there were very few fridges in British homes in wartime and as a result certain items had to be queued for and bought every day. However, there were some tricks for keeping food fresh, such as placing wet flowerpots over milk and butter to keep them cool.

To help the housewife, leaflets were printed by food producers giving ideas of recipes that could be created from the limited choice of goods available. One pointed out that 'Rationing acts as a stimulus to the cook who finds it a challenge to her ingenuity.' This is probably not how many housewives would have described the shortages. Further suggestions came in the form of cookery tips on the radio. There was only one station then, the Home Service, and at 8.15 every morning it broadcast the aptly named *Kitchen Front*. This programme gave advice on how to produce dishes without a great variety of ingredients.

There was an innovation at the BBC when *ITMA* (*It's That Man Again*) was broadcast on the radio early in the war. Although comedy shows were common on American radio, this was the first of its kind in Britain.

Although the BBC only transmitted one station, the British public did have another source of programmes to listen to. The *Germany Calling* broadcast to the UK by the Nazis was very popular, mainly because of its presenter William Joyce, better known as Lord Haw-Haw. A survey carried out estimated that by January 6 million people were listening to him. If so many were tuning in to German radio, it makes one wonder how confident those people were about the war situation.

Although air raids had not started by the beginning of the year there were already deaths among those involved in protecting the public. Two ARP wardens were found dead in a hut in Neville Road, Dagenham, by their relief team. It seems that the fumes from the stove heating the hut were responsible. Other wardens were lost from the service in the locality in the first months of 1940, but this was because of resignations: they left the ARP in protest at the lack of equipment.

At this time a string of circulars was sent out to wardens to instruct them on what to do in every eventuality. Circular 146 told them to arrange with householders to maintain supplies of water and sand for firefighting. The wardens had to know where ladders were available. (It seems they were often required to find their own equipment.) Circular 409 even set out the definition of an effective volunteer. He or she must perform a minimum of twelve hours a week post duty. Full-time wardens were also expected to serve a further twelve hours above their quota on a voluntary basis.

Opposite: A rationing recipe leaflet published by the Women's Gas Council and priced at 1*d*. These leaflets were published monthly in a series of twelve.

I pass this on to you

Preparing to get the Sunday Joint

CERTAINTIES

By JANET JOHNSTON, M.C.A.
McDougall's Cookery Expert

THE difficulties of rationing in wartime act as a stimulus to the trained cook, who finds them a challenge to her ingenuity, but to most housewives they are just another worry, like the black-out and clothing coupons. This is where the expert, whose business it is to experiment, can help the busy housewife with her rations.

The following recipes have been tested in McDougall's Experimental Kitchen, and there need be no doubt about the results if the directions are followed carefully.

PARTY CAKE	OAT CONGRESS TART
QUICKLY-MADE BREAD	CUSTARD TART
MACS CRACKERS	HOT MEAT SANDWICH
SHORT BISCUITS	NOVELTY SAVOURY PUDDING
CHEESE AND ONION PIE	

Series 8. No. 3   *Illustrated by HARRY ROUNTREE*

Only 'effective and efficient' wardens who completed training would be given uniforms. The uniform would then be seen as a symbol of their ability to do the job.

In keeping with the spirit of pulling together, some people invited servicemen into their homes. This often happened when military bases in the area had no canteen facilities. It was possible to get extra food permits from the local food office for offering this hospitality. Some householders close to military sites also gave lodging to wives who were visiting their husbands at the camps.

John Smith worked in Romford before he joined up and remembers going home for lunch to his parents' house in Brooklands Road. He found the place full of soldiers who were training at the nearby Romford Football Club ground. John's mother and some of the neighbours had clubbed together to provide tea and biscuits, which were rationed, for the soldiers after they finished drill. He recalls all the rookie conscripts running down the road to get their tea before the sergeant came to march them back to barracks.

The widespread belief nowadays has it that everyone pulled together during the war, but there were exceptions, and it was not only individuals who seem to have had a negative attitude towards helping others. The Essex Education Committee refused to let members of the public use school air-raid shelters outside school hours. The Bishop of Barking called the decision harsh but the education committee responded with the argument that if people began to use the shelters they would get used to going there all the time. Although the education committee's ruling seems severe, there were worse situations to deal with – some schools had no proper protection at all at this point in the war. In Romford parents called for deep bomb shelters for schools in the borough. Some children had been told to get under their desks during raids. Anderson shelters were available from Romford Council on easy terms – the total cost was £6 14s, but they could be bought for 25s down and 12s 6d a month.

Everyone in the country was expected to help with the war effort, even children. One way of encouraging this was the brainchild of the management of the Capitol Cinema in Barking who allowed children into the matinee for an entrance fee of bundles of salvaged paper. They loaded the paper on to a lorry parked outside.

Early in 1940 the war created some unexpected heroes. In February the Royal Navy attacked the prison ship *Altmark* off the coast of Norway and freed many British merchant seamen being held captive on board. One of the prisoners was Third Officer Leslie Frost who came from Brightlingsea. He appeared on the stage of the Regal Cinema in Colchester and was soundly cheered.

In March a new Registration of Employment Order was introduced. It applied to men over forty-one and single women of between twenty and twenty-one. (The age limit for women covered by the regulations moved upwards throughout the war.) The order meant that those to whom the rules applied could be given compulsory

Opposite: Olive Cooper and Harold Howey were married at All Saints' church in Upper Dovercourt. *(Olive Cooper)*

directions as to where they would work. They could neither leave their allocated job without permission nor be dismissed by their employer.

April brought the first Essex land casualties of the Luftwaffe when a German plane dropping magnetic mines in the Thames Estuary crashed into houses in Victoria Road, Clacton. Six died, including the crew of the aircraft, but many more were injured. This was big news to a country that had been expecting attacks by waves of bombers for months. Reporters and photographers swamped the area trying to interview survivors and workers from rescue organisations. Before long they would not have to travel so far to gather news.

It was not only reporters who rushed to the scene. Olive Cooper and her friends cycled to Clacton from Dovercourt to see the big hole left by the crash. When she later met her husband she found out that he and his friends had done the same thing.

Not everyone in the country hurried to join the forces at this time. There were some who disagreed with the war and were not prepared to fight. These men had to attend conscientious objector tribunals in law courts. They were often given the choice of joining the ARP or the Auxiliary Fire Service (AFS), or working on the land. The Essex War Agricultural Executive Committee was responsible for employing conscientious objectors on local farms. These men often laboured alongside regular agricultural workers and were paid the same wages; those doing heavy manual work were, like their colleagues, entitled to an extra ration of cheese. As in other walks of life, the reception conscientious objectors received depended entirely on the beliefs of those they worked with. Some areas also had local Pacifist Service Units. These organisations were responsible for serving hot drinks to people in public bomb shelters.

Some men did not join the forces because they were in reserved occupations. It was also possible for employers to apply for a deferment of service for employees who were vital to their industry. In addition there was a scheme by which men could apply for deferment on grounds of financial hardship.

There were others who withdrew from the war in another way: reports of suicides appeared regularly.

In May many Essex men joined the flotilla of small boats that crossed the Channel to help rescue soldiers from the beaches of Dunkirk. Many of these vessels came from Southend, including fishing boats and the town's lifeboat, the *Greater London*. Harwich also sent numerous boats across the Channel, and not only British soldiers were saved. The railway ferry *Prague* was carrying 3,000 French soldiers when it was hit. The men were rescued by a warship. Several of the ferries from Harwich were hit. Some were destroyed and many local members of their crews died. Another

Opposite: Len Cooper, Olive's brother, was in the Royal Navy. He was on HMS *Naiad* when she was torpedoed by U-boat 565 off the coast of Egypt in March 1942. Len survived but a good friend of his from Parkeston did not. *(Olive Cooper)*

source of Essex-based transport for the men stranded at Dunkirk was the paddle steamers that carried day-trippers from London to Southend in peacetime. These boats had been used to ferry evacuees earlier in the war. Many of them now went across to France and saved numerous lives. The *Royal Eagle*, owned by the General Steam & Navigation Company, made three trips to Dunkirk, and despite coming under heavy fire was responsible for saving over 3,000 men. Its sister ship, the *Crested Eagle*, was not as lucky. On its first trip it was bombed and 300 lives were lost with the vessel.

The death of local men in action was reported in the *Romford Times*, but there was no roll of honour as there had been in the First World War. A Major Milton and

IMPORTANT NOTICE
EVACUATION

The public throughout the country generally are being told to "stay put" in the event of invasion. For military reasons, however, it will in the event of attack be necessary to remove from this town all except those persons who have been specially instructed to stay. An order for the compulsory evacuation of this town will be given when in the judgment of the Government it is necessary, and plans have been arranged to give effect to such an order when it is made.

You will wish to know how you can help NOW in these plans.

THOSE WHO ARE ENGAGED IN WORK OF ANY DESCRIPTION IN THE TOWN SHOULD STAY FOR THE PRESENT.

OTHER PERSONS SHOULD, SO FAR AS THEY ARE ABLE TO DO SO, MAKE ARRANGEMENTS TO LEAVE THE TOWN—PARTICULARLY
MOTHERS WITH YOUNG CHILDREN
SCHOOL CHILDREN
AGED AND INFIRM PERSONS
PERSONS WITHOUT OCCUPATION OR IN RETIREMENT.

All such persons who can arrange for their accommodation with relatives or friends in some other part of the country should do so. Assistance for railway fares and accommodation will be given to those who require it.

Advice and, where possible, assistance will be given to persons who desire to leave the town but are unable to make their own arrangements.

Information about these matters can be obtained from the local Council Offices.

(*Signed*) WILL SPENS,
Regional Commissioner for Civil Defence.
CAMBRIDGE,
2nd July, 1940.

(393/4177) Wt. 19544-30 125M 7/40 H & S Ltd. **Gp. 393**

An evacuation leaflet handed out to the public with instructions on what to do in the event of invasion. There were also more area-specific leaflets which included evacuation routes and other local information.

a Captain Westley, both of Romford, were reported missing while fighting in the rearguard at Dunkirk.

Deaths of military personnel did not only occur overseas. Tragic accidents claimed lives at home, too. A young Romford man, who had been married only ten weeks, was killed in Wiltshire. Jack Bannister of Victoria Road died when his motorbike hit a kerb while he was serving with the Military Police. Meanwhile, an eighteen-year-old WAAF, Dorothy Calder from Chadwell Heath, died in Leighton Buzzard trying to stop a runaway car with six children in it.

The defences at Beacon Hill Fort in Harwich had been expanded to three 6-inch guns by this time. The guns were protected by concrete roofs to guard against air attack. These roof platforms carried Bofors anti-aircraft guns. A radar tower had also been added to the fort.

In May Harry Channon MP, a junior minister at the Foreign Office, was living at Kelvedon. He obviously did not have much faith in his government and its ability to fight the war. He was a great diary writer and was worried that the information in his journals might fall into enemy hands. He decided to put them in a tin box and bury them by the west wall of the churchyard at Kelvedon for safekeeping, along with some other valuables.

Another force of volunteers was raised in May when Sir Anthony Eden, the Secretary of State for War, appealed for men between seventeen and sixty-five to join the Local Defence Volunteers (LDV). For many months the members of the force had no weapons apart from what they could improvise. Although the plan was to give them uniforms and weapons, the first priority was to supply the regular army, so they had to wait.

Essex has a great tradition of raising voluntary forces in times of crisis and this war was no different. The County of Essex Volunteer Force was unofficial but already numbered 400 men by the time Eden asked for volunteers to form the LDV. The idea of a volunteer force had also been put forward before Eden's appeal by the Bishop of Chelmsford in the *Diocesan Chronicle*. He said that town guards should be enrolled to patrol vital buildings such as power stations, gasworks and waterworks.

In Chelmsford men rushed to join the Sixth Essex Battalion, which was an LDV unit based in Springfield Hill. If the threatened invasion came, their first task was to destroy the Esso petrol depot in Victoria Road to stop the fuel falling into enemy hands. They were not the only volunteer force in the town. The Post Office staff formed the 35th GPO Battalion. It was commanded by the town's head postmaster, Lieutenant-Colonel Gaze, and had a strength of 650 men. In Romford the newly formed Local Defence Volunteers paraded at the dog track in June. Some were in uniform and wearing medals won in the First World War. They were reviewed by Brigadier-General Charlton, the local inspector of the LDV.

One of the prime objectives of the Local Defence Volunteers was to deal with enemy parachutists. Because any landing by this method would be likely to take place in the countryside, the government decided to concentrate on organising and arming these areas first. King George VI carried out the first royal inspection of the Local Defence Volunteers at Woodford in July.

The war did not put an end to pleasant walks through the Castle Park in Colchester. If there was an air raid then the castle vaults were close by to use as a shelter.

There was a great deal of disappointment in Colchester at the delay in forming an LDV unit. It was not one of the priority areas and in addition it was already a garrison town with a large military presence. However, several complaints were made by the men of Colchester to the authorities in Chelmsford and it was finally agreed that a limited force of 200 could be raised in the town. Choosing these men was difficult because by then there had been over 1,000 volunteers. To qualify as an officer, a man had to conform to certain requirements, such as having a telephone and some form of transport to ensure a rapid turn out in an emergency. This inevitably meant that officers came from the better-off section of the population.

Although most LDV units were linked to particular geographical areas, some were organised to look after very specific locations. One of these was the May & Baker Detachment, formed at the government's request to protect the Dagenham site. During training the volunteers were told to protect the factory from an attack by paratroopers based at Hornchurch. While the unit defended the rear of the factory, the paras attacked the front but were driven off by the works fire brigade using hoses.

There was a great deal of disappointment among many men who had already rushed to volunteer for civil defence duties: officially, no one already serving in one of the other civil organisations could also enrol in the Local Defence Volunteers. In reality there was a degree of leeway in the system and some men managed to do both jobs at the same time. The rules were later changed to allow for this.

Churchill was quick to make a speech praising the new volunteer force. His description of an army bristling with defiance and bayonets may have been an overestimation, however. Very few of the volunteers even owned a bayonet. No doubt the prime minister was hoping that the content of his speech would reach the ears of Hitler who was unaware of the LDV's lack of weapons.

The fall of France on 24 June 1940 led to grave fears of invasion, which meant preparations had to be made in coastal areas. Great Wakering received a visit from the commandant of nearby Shoebury Barracks. He asked that an invasion committee be formed to ensure that important services were maintained if the Germans landed. Rations were to be stored in secret locations and wells made ready to provide alternative water supplies. The church hall became a store for papier mâché coffins and plans were made for roads to be kept clear in the event of an invasion.

Fear of invasion led to panic among some of the population and rumours of spies were rife. One hotel owner in Colchester took out an advertisement in the local press to deny that he had been arrested because secret radio equipment had been found in his premises. Another rumour had it that Lord Haw-Haw had announced the town hall clock was two minutes slow, revealing what good knowledge the Germans had of the county. This seems to have been a popular story – towns in many parts of the country had their own versions, always without any basis in fact whatsoever.

Panic led to incidents that now seem to have been long forgotten. Two army sentries and a policeman were checking vehicles on an Essex road when a car carrying five men drove past, refusing to stop. The sentries opened fire and the driver and the passenger in the front seat were wounded.

At this time road names and town directions were removed from signboards everywhere. Some even believed that gravestones marked 'late of' followed by the name of the town should be taken down. In Chelmsford the signs were dismantled in June, including street names that were clues to the direction in which other towns lay, for example Colchester Road.

In the same month Essex came under the restrictions of the Aliens Order. This led to twenty regular stallholders in Romford Market being banned from trading. Many of them were local men, the rest being from East London, but none of them were British citizens.

The original mobile anti-aircraft site at Bowater's Farm, East Tilbury, had been replaced by permanent emplacements of four 4.5-inch guns by now. Magazines were also built and searchlights were added. The shortage of weapons meant that many of the guns mounted as coastal defences were of First World War vintage.

By June hundreds of Romford people still did not have access to an air-raid shelter. The council took over unused land to build more, but they had to be locked at night because they became dossing areas for tramps. Not all Essex town councils were so quick off the mark. In Chelmsford there was a shortage of public air-raid shelters due to the scarcity of bricks and cement. Further restrictions put in place by the government meant that the town's council was only allowed to build shelters for 10 per cent of the population.

Although June was the beginning of summer, trips to the seaside had become a thing of the past. Southend was declared an evacuation area and children from the town's schools were sent off to the Midlands. The youngsters gathered at Southend station before sunrise for an emotional departure. Over 8,000 were watched by tearful parents as they boarded trains waiting in sidings. The scene was presided over by the mayor and other civic dignitaries. The first train left at 7 a.m. followed by others at half-hourly intervals. The town's schools were then closed. It was not only the young who left. A number of the adult population also quit Southend. The beach was fenced with barbed wire and many of the seafront buildings were boarded up or taken over by the army. Along with most other Essex seaside towns, Southend became almost deserted for the duration of the war.

Harwich was expected to be an even greater target than most other coastal towns. The children and many adults departed, leaving the army, navy and the Local Defence Volunteers to wait for the expected invasion. The beaches were closed for much of the war.

By the end of the month it was not only coastal resorts that had become no-go areas. The land east of the A130 from Canvey Island to Chelmsford became a restricted zone. It was covered in pillboxes and tank-traps.

The war had another, more unexpected, effect on the coast of Essex. Because of the build-up of ships in the Thames and the constant threat of enemy attack, it was decided to move the Artillery School from Shoeburyness to Wales. It was the first time in eighty years that Shoeburyness had been without an artillery school.

Also in June the Germans invaded the Channel Islands. This led to a shortage of onions, which had been supplied from there in large numbers. At the same time an onion blight struck on the mainland. The vegetables became so rare that they were offered as prizes in competitions and even given as gifts.

In July two guns from HMS *Hood* were mounted at Coalhouse Fort in East Tilbury, a defence that dates back to the mid-nineteenth century in its present form. Some older guns had already been sited at the fort after the First World War.

In July, too, Winston Churchill applied his great mind to the problem of the Local Defence Volunteers. He did not like the name and changed it to the much more professional-sounding Home Guard. By this time the force numbered over a million men.

The month also finally saw the beginning of the expected onslaught by the Luftwaffe. Bombing commenced in London and parts of Essex, causing damage to both industrial and residential buildings. The start of sustained bombing quickly revealed the shortcomings in government provision for victims. Rest centres for those bombed out were often in school buildings and the government expected victims quickly to move on to other accommodation they had arranged themselves.

The Ford Motor Company in Dagenham suffered numerous attacks like this one in October 1940, but production continued. *(Ford Motor Company)*

This was not always an option, but the rest centres were not equipped for long-term occupation. There were few sanitary facilities and not even many blankets or much first-aid equipment. It was only the hard work of volunteers that made the centres anywhere near habitable.

Another effect of the bombing for which the government was unprepared was orphaned children. In several cases a child survived a direct hit when his or her parents did not. The responsibility for these children was quickly passed on to the Women's Voluntary Service which would arrange to evacuate the victims.

Evacuation was not always the safe option that people believed it to be, however. Four-year-old John Stobart from Romford was killed when the house he was staying in was bombed. The house, in the Midlands, was reported to have collapsed like a pack of cards. The boy's mother was in bed with him but survived. His father was serving in the navy.

There were regular official requests for scrap of various kinds throughout the war. Sometimes it seemed that the appeals were either badly organised or had perhaps

Another attack on Ford. Because of its position on the River Thames, the works was on the route many bombers followed to London. *(Ford Motor Company)*

been begun for reasons other than a shortage of material. At the height of the Battle of Britain there were calls for aluminium, which was needed to build more planes. The kitchens of Essex, along with those of the rest of the country, were stripped of saucepans, kettles and any other item made of the metal. However, while every household made the sacrifice, aluminium items were still on sale in the shops and scrap merchants also had supplies of the material. The actual amount collected in appeals probably had little effect on the war effort, but it had a direct impact on morale because everyone felt he or she was doing their bit to help.

An even more direct way of supporting the war effort was to donate cash, although how that was supposed to help if there were no materials to buy was not explained. Many towns raised enough to meet the cost of a Spitfire, priced at £5,000, but there were cheaper items which could be bought by individuals. A bomb could be paid for with as little as £20. What better way to help the war effort than actually to purchase something that was going to destroy enemy materiel or even personnel?

July 1940 saw the first prosecution in Romford for failing to immobilise a car – a new wartime offence intended to prevent vehicles falling into enemy hands. The driver left the key in the ignition of his vehicle when it was parked in Romford marketplace. He argued in court that there were two dogs in the car who were guarding it, but he was still fined 10*s*.

The following month saw the beginning of concentrated attacks by the enemy on RAF airfields. One of the Germans' favourite bombers was the Heinkel He111. This aircraft had been very successful in the conquest of the rest of Europe. Against the RAF, however, it was shown to be too slow and it became easy prey to British fighters. In one attack aimed at North Weald and Hornchurch Airfields thirty-six Heinkels, fifty Dorniers and a flight of Me109s and 110s headed across the Channel. They were met by six Hurricanes from North Weald and another nine from Kenley. Despite the outrageous odds, the Hurricanes were instrumental in forcing many of the bombers to drop their weapons before they reached their targets. This had an adverse effect on the people of Essex but it stopped a major attack on the airfields. During one raid on North Weald a shelter took a direct hit and nine men from the Essex Regiment, who were based at the airfield, were killed.

Even if the father of a family was not in the forces, he would often be absent for periods during the war. Peter Russell was eight when the conflict began and lived in Beauchamp Roding near Ongar. He recalls that his father was often away at night because he was an air-raid warden in Maldon. Peter's home was close to North Weald RAF Fighter Command station and so he often had to endure air raids. He remembers that his mother had to rush around putting out incendiary devices and that the family always slept downstairs.

A LAST APPEAL TO REASON

BY

ADOLF HITLER

Speech before the Reichstag, 19th July, 1940

I have summoned you to this meeting in the midst of our tremendous struggle for the freedom and the future of the German nation. I have done so, firstly, because I considered it imperative to give our own people an insight into the events, unique in history, that lie behind us, secondly, because I wished to express my gratitude to our magnificent soldiers, and thirdly, with the intention of appealing, once more and for the last time, to common sense in general.

If we compare the causes which prompted this historic struggle with the magnitude and the far-reaching effects of military events, we are forced to the conclusion that its general course and the sacrifices it has entailed are out of all proportion to the alleged reasons for its outbreak — unless they were nothing but a pretext for underlying intentions.

the world our resolution to shake off the shackles of the Versailles Dictate.

Germany's demands for this revision were a vital necessity and essential to the existence and honour of every great nation. They will probably one day be regarded by posterity as extremely reasonable. In practice, all these demands had to be carried through contrary to the will of the Franco-British rulers. We all regarded it as a sure sign of successful leadership in the Third Reich that for years we were able to effect this revision without a war. Not that — as the British and French demagogues asserted — we were at that time incapable of fighting. When, thanks to growing common sense, it finally appeared as though international co-operation might lead to a peaceful solution of the remaining problems, the Agreement to this end signed in Munich on September 29, 1938, by the four leading interested States was not only not welcomed in

needed a long war, because they had now invested their capital in armaments shares, had purchased machinery and required time for the development of their business interests and the amortisation of their investments. For, after all, what do these "citizens of the world" care about Poles, Czechs or such-like peoples?

On June 19, 1940, a German soldier found a curious document when searching some railway trucks standing in the station of La Charité. As the document bore a distinctive inscription, he immediately handed it over to his commanding officer. It was then passed on to other quarters, where it was soon realized that we had lighted on an important discovery. The station was subjected to another, more thorough-going search.

Thus it was that the German High Command gained possession of a collection of documents of unique historical significance. They

The front page of an English version of a speech by Hitler containing claims that documents had been found giving the plans of the warmongers of the Allied powers who wanted to extend the conflict. The report of the speech was dropped by the Germans over southern England in the form of a newspaper.

Last Appeal to Reason

In this hour I feel it to be my duty before my own conscience to appeal once more to reason and common sense, in Great Britain as much as elsewhere. I consider myself in a position to make this appeal since I am not the vanquished begging favours, but the victor speaking in the name of reason. I can see no reason why this war must go on.

I am grieved to think of the sacrifices which it will claim. I should like to avert them, also from my own people. I know that millions of German men, young and old alike, are burning with the desire at last to settle accounts with the enemy, who for the second time has declared war upon us for no reason whatever. But I also know that at home there are many women and mothers, who, ready as they are to sacrifice all they have in life, are yet bound to it by their very heart-strings.

Possibly Mr Churchill will again brush aside this statement of mine by saying that it is merely born of fear and of doubt in our final victory. In that case I shall have relieved my conscience in regard to the things to come.

Deputies and Members of the German Reichstag!

In looking back upon the last ten months we are all struck by the grace of Providence, which has allowed us to succeed in our great work. Providence has blessed our resolves and guided us on our difficult paths. As for myself, I am deeply moved, realizing that Providence has called upon me to restore to my people their freedom and honour. The humiliation and disgrace, which originated twenty-two years ago in the Forest of Compiègne, have for ever been obliterated in the same place. Today I have named before history the men who made it possible for me to accomplish this great task. All of them have given their best, and have devoted all their faculties and energy to the German people. Let me conclude by mentioning those unknown heroes, who have fulfilled their duty in no less a degree; millions of them risked life and limb and were at every moment prepared, as true German officers and soldiers, to bring for their people the greatest sacrifice of which man is capable. Many of them now lie buried side by side with their fathers, who fell in the Great War. They bear witness to a silent heroism. They are the symbol of those hundreds of thousands of infantrymen, tank corps men, engineers and gunners, sailors, airmen and SS-men, and of all those other soldiers who joined in the fight of the German Forces for the freedom and future of our people, and for the eternal greatness of the National-Socialist Reich.

A page of Hitler's 'Last Appeal to Reason' claims that the Allies had declared war on Germany for no reason whatsoever. With so much public interest shown in the views of Lord Haw-Haw, one wonders what effect these leaflets had on those who read them.

In common with other youngsters, Peter found the war a bit of an adventure. He recollects German bombers being shot down close to his home and landmines hanging from trees. Peter followed the wartime boyhood craze of collecting shrapnel, bullets and bits of bombs. Despite his age, he also helped a nearby farmer with harvesting, no doubt a great help during manpower shortages.

The local press reported air raids and even printed photographs of the damage. One story explained how a British pilot parachuted from his damaged plane and was threatened by a mob when he landed because they thought he was a German. He was rescued by the Home Guard and the police, and was taken away in an RAF truck. Although these events were reported, their location was not. They could have taken place in any town in Essex. A similar incident – perhaps the same one – is remembered by John Smith. He was at home in Romford one day when the sirens sounded. John's father said, 'There you are. Those Germans won't hesitate.' A plane flew over but turned out to be 'one of ours'. A few days later there was a sound of gunfire and everyone rushed into the street to see a parachute coming down. The crowd thought the parachutist was German and one neighbour said, 'It must be some poor mother's son.' John's father only had one leg because of his First World War wounds and he waved his crutch and shouted, 'I'll give him mother's son if he lands here.' The man with the parachute turned out to be British. He landed somewhere near Rush Green in Romford and John later heard that the police needed to protect him from an irate but misguided crowd.

Stanley Holmes, MP for Harwich, reported after a visit to the town that the government was delighted with the spirit of the population. The idea that everyone was still pulling together was, however, sometimes shaken. A letter to the editor in the *Essex County Standard* reported how a woman with two children was caught outside in an air raid and asked a householder standing at her front door if they could come in. The woman refused, telling the mother that she was not running a public shelter.

The story brings home the difficulty of performing the simplest tasks. Even a shopping trip could be fraught with danger. An air raid which occurred when shops were crowded could lead to panic. If people were away from their own area then it was possible they would not know where the shelters were. Fortunately, many shops with basements would open them up to customers in such a situation.

Although the morale of the public was said to be good, this was not always the full story. There is a belief that the cheerful cockneys of London's East End and the people who lived in the parts of Essex that the docks spread to went through the war with a grin and a joke as the bombs rained down on them. When the heaviest bombing started in the East End, however, many were very angry. They felt that not enough was being done to help them. Many inhabitants of areas close to the docks did not grin and bear it; they fled to the relative safety of places like Epping Forest, which became a large campsite for refugees running from the havoc caused by continual German raids. West Ham became almost a ghost town because so many of the population left. At one time the army used the streets for training because they were so empty.

The beginning of widespread bombing meant that civilians were now just as likely to be killed as the men fighting in the forces. Most of the damage that occurred in Essex towns was due to planes disposing of the remains of their load on the way back from raids in London. Bombing brought not only death but also serious injury, leading to a rise in the disabled population. There was also an increasing tide of homelessness. The lucky ones had friends or family to stay with. Others were eventually found a place to live by the local authorities. Some had no option but to remain in damaged buildings. But there was not only the loss of a person's home to consider. Often everything the bomb victim owned was also destroyed. The resulting payment from the government in compensation only reimbursed the loss of furniture, not luxuries. Dockets were given to allow those with nothing to buy some furniture but often most of what was available was second-hand from house auctions.

Those who did not live through it cannot imagine how anyone could cope with an air raid, especially a young woman with children whose husband was off serving in the forces. Every time there was an alarm a mother had to decide whether or not to get the children out of bed. If there was a baby in the house then bottles, nappies and all the other paraphernalia had to be taken to the shelter too. Some people were so frightened that they actually tried to live in shelters.

When the raid was over, occupants of shelters could come out to find the area had changed beyond recognition. Those who had not reached the shelters were frequently still visible to the emerging public: body parts were often scattered in the road.

In hospitals patients had to be carried into the shelters on stretchers. The same problem occurred with residents of old people's homes.

Many homes had their own Anderson shelter in the garden. Others had a Morrison shelter in the house. Although many used Morrison shelters as tables and then climbed into them when there was a raid, the more enterprising used them as beds with a mattress on top. If this technique was adopted it was possible to get straight out of bed and into the shelter when there was a night raid.

It is easy to look at the number of those killed by the bombing and forget that each death caused personal tragedy for the victim's friends and family. Only when a name and a story are put to a fatality does it become real. Such is the case of Grace

COUNTY BOROUGH OF SOUTHEND - ON - SEA.

AIR RAID PRECAUTIONS DEPARTMENT.

Y/S.
Circ. No. 360.

120 Victoria Avenue,
Southend-on-Sea.

August 29th 1940.

CLOUD GAS ATTACK FROM THE SEA.

The possibility of such an attack must not be overlooked.

The Military in the event of such an attack will sound the alarm using a striker on a suspended rail with a series of rapid strokes in order to avoid confusion with Church bells.

As regards the Wardens Service, the relay of this alarm by rattles should not be given unless gas is actually detected.

It is thought that Phosgene and Chlorine would be the gases most likely to be used in such an attack.

I shall be obliged if you will make this known to the personnel attached to your post or unit, but see that it is not relayed to the public.

Air Raid Precautions Officer.

TO:

Post Commanders - Air Raid Wardens Service.
Senior Riders   - Despatch Service.

A warden's letter explaining how the alarm for a gas attack would differ from the sound of church bells.

Ethel Dean from Barking and her husband Deric Carter from Plumstead. They were married in St Margaret's church in Barking just before the war. Their daughter Christine was born in 1939. Deric joined the army when the war started but then transferred to the RAF and was posted to Biggin Hill. He was killed during an attack on the airbase in August 1940, leaving his daughter of one year old to grow up without knowing her father.

Industry was hit by the bombing. Ford's factory at Dagenham was targeted on a number of occasions but production was not badly delayed. The Howard chemical works in Ilford was also bombed and one of the directors, James Howard, and a number of workers were killed. Plessey at Ilford was carrying out war work when it was hit. The company then set up a production line in the underground railway tunnel between Wanstead and Gants Hill.

Although there might have not been much to travel for, apart from evacuation, anyone who did try to move around the country was advised to take precautions, including carrying enough food to last for twenty-four hours. This warning prompted stores to advertise that they could provide the food needed for trips. (Many other businesses were not averse to using the war as a means of selling their goods, too – seed merchants were forever using advertising to tell the population how important it was to grow your own food.)

Wartime travel could certainly be a challenge; even the morning journey to work might be beset by numerous hurdles. Railway lines were often damaged in night-time raids, preventing trains from running for days. So many buses were destroyed that it was not unusual for queues at stops to consist of huge numbers of people. Trolley buses were even more prone to damage as they needed overhead wires for power. For a time, travel problems between Essex and London were eased by a boat service running on the Thames.

Essex was strewn with crashed enemy planes as the Spitfires and Hurricanes took a terrible toll on German bombers. One well-documented battle in 1940 involved a Heinkel that was shot down over Maldon. Two of the crew bailed out and were visible from the ground as they came down by parachute. The rest died as the plane crashed into the ground near Heybridge. Between fifty and sixty people arrived at the crash site – it was normal for the public to try to get a souvenir of downed enemy aircraft. The sightseers were followed by the military who arrived later and defused several bombs that had landed without detonating. Then came someone from the Air Ministry, which logged the site of all the enemy aircraft brought down in Britain. One of the surviving crew members was found by a soldier who was on leave. He rode on his bicycle towards where the German had come down. Despite being unarmed he approached the airman, who was badly hurt, and stayed with him until an ARP warden arrived.

There was a reminder of Essex military connections from the past when, in July, representatives of the East India Company presented eight Spitfires and a cheque for £55,000 towards more planes for Hornchurch Airfield. These aircraft were named the East India Squadron. The company had owned nearby Warley Barracks for part of the nineteenth century when it had its own army to keep order in India.

COUNTY BOROUGH OF SOUTHEND-ON-SEA.
AIR RAID PRECAUTIONS DEPARTMENT.

120 Victoria Avenue,
Southend-on-Sea.

Y/S.
Circ. No. 367.   September 12th 1940.

WAR DAMAGE TO PROPERTY.
FOOD SHOPS - WHOLESALE AND RETAIL.

        I shall be obliged if you will indicate on your Reports
of War Damage to property those premises which are Food Shops.

        This information is required in order to enable the
Food Executive Officer to make immediate arrangements for the
provision of food stuffs to the registered customers.

AIR RAID PRECAUTIONS OFFICER.

TO:
        THE AIR RAID WARDEN SERVICE.

The bombing of a food shop could have serious consequences for those registered with the store for their rations, hence the instructions to wardens to report such attacks.

A little-known arm of the Home Guard was formed without public knowledge at this time. The British Resistance Organisation was such a well-kept secret that its existence did not become common knowledge until well after the end of the war. Its members were not released from their secrecy vow until 1966. Even their wives were unaware of their job. Their mission was to hide in the event of invasion, then to come out and harass the invading force from behind. Units consisted of around six men who all had a good knowledge of the local area. One such group was enlisted in Weeley. They were part of 203 Battalion Home Guard. A hideout was built in Weeley Hall Wood. Orders for the group were left in a drainpipe. After an invasion scare at Harwich the group spent two days in their hideout.

In 1940 the coroner at Colchester was told how one soldier died through sheer bad luck. The 23-year-old contracted blood poisoning which originated in a blister caused by his army boots. In Clacton an army sergeant was found guilty of breaking into a house and stealing blankets and sheets, but he could not give any explanation as to why he had done it.

Crime was also still a problem among the civilian population but the war was having an effect on the type of offence committed. In Stratford two men were found guilty of stealing air-raid shelters from their employer, Leyton Borough Council. At Brentwood two brothers were sent to prison for a month for refusing to comply with the national registration regulations. Another wartime crime led to a woman being sent to prison in Clacton. She was charged with trying to cause disaffection. She told some soldiers not to get involved in a war that was nothing to do with them and advised them to revolt. The woman was described as a follower of George Bernard Shaw and Oswald Mosley. She was sentenced to three months.

The first sign of the enemy in the Havering area came when a German plane was shot down and the pilot was captured in Hornchurch in September. One of the worst early raids in Romford occurred at roughly the same time when over forty mines were dropped around Stanley Avenue.

September was not a good month for the religious communities of two Essex towns. On the 16th St Peter's church at Coggeshall was hit and damaged by a bomb that landed in the churchyard. On the 21st a parachute mine hit the parish church at Little Horkesley. The historic building was completely destroyed.

September also saw a change in circumstances in Colchester. The town had been designated an evacuation reception centre, then a neutral centre, and was now an evacuation centre. The same staff who had been responsible for welcoming evacuees were now in control of sending them away. Not only children but also the elderly and even many women departed, leaving behind an army of lonely husbands.

Not all the heroes of the war were serving overseas. In September 1940 an enormous magnetic mine was dropped in the River Roding at Barking, very close to the power station. If it had exploded it could have caused severe damage to the station and disrupted the war effort in the surrounding area. Lieutenant John Duppa-Miller of the Royal Naval Volunteer Reserve and Able Seaman Stephen Tuckwell RN defused the device. It had a 20-second fuse which, if activated, would have given the men no chance of getting clear. Both were awarded the George Cross.

Not far from the site of Duppa-Millar and Tuckwell's heroism another example of bravery occurred, this time by civilians, and it also led to the award of medals. Incendiary bombs started a large fire at the May & Baker chemical works in Dagenham. The burning material was sodium, which becomes even more dangerous when sprayed with water. The local fire brigade arrived and despite being informed of the difficulties of the situation by the works firefighters, they prepared to use their water hoses. One of the works firemen, L. Fisher, reputedly knocked out the fireman in charge and took control himself. Fisher and another works fireman, W. Beeson, put out the blaze using cement powder. They were both awarded the George Medal.

September 1940 was the month in which invasion was expected. Every available weapon was utilised to defend the country. Members of a unit of the Essex Regiment were given new equipment which they set up on the sea wall at Canvey Island – the weapons were Maxim Guns dating from the turn of the century and more suited to a museum than a modern war. By the end of the month, however, Hitler had realised that he had not managed to destroy the RAF. Every large German air attack was still met with dogged resistance by fighters from the many airfields in Essex and other parts of the country. The Germans now knew that invasion was not an option at this time and their plans were soon cancelled.

Joan Francis of Thorpe-le-Soken remembers her first encounter with a bomb. One fell on a field while the family hid in the cupboard under the stairs. The next morning a victim lay in the crater – a cow that had been blown up to an enormous size by its internal gases. Joan's mother decided that this was a warning and sent the younger children off to friends in Derbyshire. On another evening Joan and her mother heard an explosion and learnt that an enemy plane had crashed on Clacton's recreation ground. The crew were given a honourable funeral.

Joan and her boyfriend would walk the country lanes in the evening watching searchlights as they caught planes in their crossed beams. They were told that the aircraft were flying low over the coast on their way to bomb Coventry. They could hear shrapnel dropping all around them, but like other young people during the conflict, they did not feel that they were in any danger. The next day they would go out to see how much shrapnel they could collect. Some evenings they would cycle into Clacton to go to the cinema and often met air-raid wardens, also on bicycles, blowing their whistles to warn of raids. Joan and her boyfriend ignored the wardens' warnings.

During a raid on Dagenham on 21 September a parachute mine landed on a house in Oval Road North. Jimmy Underwood lived nearby and remembers the Hall family who owned it. According to the story Jimmy heard, Mr Hall sat up in bed and hit his head on the mine as it hung through the bedroom ceiling. Miraculously, the family got out of the house safely. The incident is also recalled by Ted Slade who lived nearby. He was told that bomb-disposal men went into the house and as they opened a door it hit the mine that was hanging behind it which then exploded and killed them. The men were Chief Petty Officer Reg Vincent Ellingworth and Lieutenant-Commander Richard Ryan. They were both posthumously awarded the George Cross.

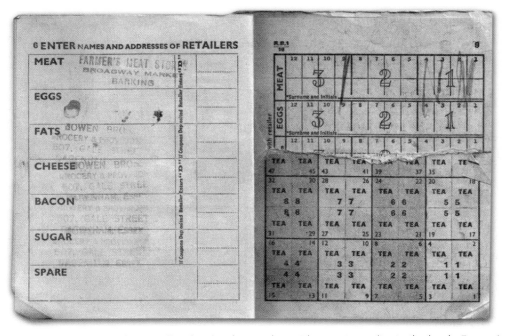

A ration book for one of the Walker family of Dagenham. The meat supplier in the book, Farmer's Meat Store in Barking, is still in business. (*Sylvia Walker*)

Ted Slade has memories of his own home being bombed, more than once. The house his family rented in Whitebarn Lane, Dagenham, was damaged so they went to stay with a relative in Brixton. They caught a train from Dagenham Heathway and Ted recollects that it travelled slowly so as not to make any sparks. He also recalls an enemy plane following the train as it headed towards London. The Slade family later returned to Dagenham to live in a house in New Road. This was hit by an anti-aircraft shell and they had to move again, this time to Review Road.

Ted remembers the war as an adventure; grown-ups, he says, were more frightened. One night he stood by the Princess Cinema in Dagenham and watched the oil refineries at Canvey Island burn. The area where part of Ford's works now stands was then open fields and it was possible to see out towards the Thames Estuary. The light from the flames was so strong that he could have read a newspaper by it, despite the fact that it was evening and the blackout was in force.

In Dagenham itself it was not only houses that were hit. The diving board at Leys open-air swimming pool was damaged during a raid. This did not stop Jimmy Underwood and his friends from climbing over the wall at night to use the pool.

Despite a decreasing threat of invasion, a curfew was put in force on the east coast. It stretched from the Wash to Southend and 5 miles inland. It lasted from an hour after sunset to an hour before sunrise. Access to beaches was restricted at any time unless expressly allowed by the local military authority. There were further problems for councils in coastal areas. They applied to the government for financial help because they lost so much in rates when large sections of the local population left.

In October the stationmaster at Weeley was woken in the middle of the night by a surprising visitor. A German airman knocked on the door. By the time the stationmaster got to the door the man had gone, but he and the rest of his crew from a crashed bomber were later arrested. The Thames coast was frequently overflown by large numbers of German aircraft on their way to bomb London. By the time they returned they were often being pursued by RAF fighters and many came down along the Thames and close to the sea, so many in fact that German aircrews became a regular sight in the area. A daily train from Shoeburyness to Fenchurch Street always had a carriage reserved for German prisoners. It was not always the Home Guard or the military who caught enemy airmen. A porter at South Ockendon station was approached by a man in November. He turned out to be a German airman and he was still carrying his pistol. The German handed over his gun and surrendered.

The heaviest bombing to hit Romford during the Battle of Britain occurred in October and November 1940. In October a public shelter was hit, the only incident of its kind in the town during the war, and six people were killed. In November the average number of casualties per damaged house rose from one to three. As the town was outside the defences for London there were no anti-aircraft guns in the area in the early days of the war. The nearest were in fields next to Whalebone Lane in Dagenham.

The mayor of Chelmsford was killed in an air raid in October. John Thompson, his wife and several members of his family died when a bomb landed on their home.

Air-raid shelters were necessary at hospitals but it must have been very difficult to get patients into them. This is the last example of a shelter at Oldchurch Hospital in Romford, now bricked up and overgrown.

In the same month the Australians arrived in Essex to help fight the Germans. They marched into Colchester, if their relaxed gait could be called marching. A band playing 'Waltzing Matilda' led them, and they carried on as though they were in a parade. Wearing hats that Essex people had only seen in westerns at the cinema, they did not look like any soldiers the locals had encountered before. The arrival of these happy, carefree men raised the morale of the crowds who lined the streets to welcome them. The Australians were soon followed by New Zealanders, Canadians and even Indians, who came leading lines of packhorses. It was to be their job to operate in terrain where vehicles could not go.

Of those foreign soldiers who arrived in 1940, the Canadians were to have the biggest effect on the local population. Over 500 of them returned home after the war taking brides from Essex with them. Only the Americans, who came later, succeeded in securing a greater number of Essex wives.

November saw a new phenomenon in the skies over the county. Although officially the Battle of Britain was over, there were still constant bombing raids, mainly at night. It was after dark that pilots from Hornchurch were called out to meet a raid and found themselves facing Italian planes. Mussolini had sent a small part of his air force to help the Germans fight the RAF. This consisted of Fiat biplanes, which were totally outclassed by the Spitfire. Italian involvement in the fight for Britain's skies was very short-lived.

FOUR

1941: Free Orange Juice and Cheap Restaurants

The arrival of Australian support helped the Allies gain the advantage in the deserts of North Africa and they took Tobruk from the Italians on 12 January 1941. Unfortunately, the need to bolster the Italian Army finally prompted the Germans to become involved in the conflict in this part of the world, and in April the Allied war in the desert took a turn for the worse as Rommel began to succeed where the Italians had failed. The Australians occupying Tobruk came under months of sustained bombardment. The Allies retaliated with an attempt to assassinate Rommel but he had flown to Rome by the time the squad arrived to get him. (After a long siege Tobruk was retaken by the Germans in 1942.)

In Europe the Germans seemed to be moving forward at an alarming rate. In April 1941 combined German, Italian, Hungarian and Bulgarian forces attacked Yugoslavia and in the same month British troops were evacuated from Greece as German forces invaded. By the beginning of 1941 the 'free' governments of over a dozen occupied countries were in exile in London.

March marked the beginning of the US Lend-Lease Act and extra supplies began to flow across the Atlantic from the United States. Food was in seriously short supply by this time, and pets could no longer be fed on anything that was fit for human consumption.

May saw the unexpected arrival of Rudolf Hess in Scotland. The capture of the deputy leader of the Nazi Party led to speculation that he was there to offer peace terms, a suggestion that both sides denied. In June the German invasion of Russia – Operation Barbarossa – began. Although some Russians suspected the Germans had such plans, they did not believe the invasion would really happen. Hitler's decision to go ahead with Barbarossa took some of the pressure off Britain as German aircraft were moved to the Eastern Front. August saw a decline in the number of vessels claimed by U-boats.

In 1941 the Air Training Corps was formed to assist the war effort and to help keep young people busy. It was open to those aged between sixteen and eighteen, and the idea was later extended to form Naval and Army Training Corps. This gave young people an interesting place to go after work or school.

In December the Americans put pressure on the Japanese to withdraw from China. In retaliation the Japanese attacked Pearl Harbor with the result that America was at last drawn into the war.

The year 1941 heralded the beginning of travel restrictions on the people of Essex. A 10-mile exclusion area was set up along the coast and no unauthorised person was allowed into it. There had to be some exceptions, however, because local people had to be allowed to use certain areas for shopping. A woman who enquired whether she could visit Colchester library was told she could not, but she was allowed to go to the shops.

The threat of sudden death was a constant companion throughout the war, not only for men serving in the forces but for their families at home. A snowfall in January encouraged excited children to go out to play: two young girls doing just that were killed by a German bomb in North Stifford. Two whole families were wiped out in what the newspapers called 'an Essex coastal town'. The town was not named, of course, but the *Essex County Standard* reported how a plane circled overhead before dropping its bombs on a working-class district. The bombs blew out of the ground four Anderson shelters situated in adjoining gardens. The families sleeping inside two of the shelters were killed.

For children, wartime experiences were not all bad. Free orange juice was introduced to attempt to alleviate the damage done to young bodies by a restricted diet, although, unfortunately for the children, it was accompanied by cod liver oil. Free milk was also given out, initially to the poorest, but then the scheme was extended to all school pupils, each of whom received a bottle a day.

Some children certainly had a difficult time, but it is debatable whether this was due to the war or to their school's regime. Peter Russell was sent away from his home near Ongar to attend Harlow College, which was a boarding school. He remembers that it was very strict. The boys were allowed out of school once a week for an hour. They received pocket money of 2*s* a week, which Peter always spent on food because he was so hungry. The boys sometimes slept in the school dormitory but would often spend the night in the air-raid shelter or in a covered part of the playground during good weather. Peter would count the days until the end of term because he missed home so much. He was continually worried about friends and family, and missed the freedom he had at home, as well as the food. At night he would listen to a crystal set in bed, hoping to get some news of home. He also received regular letters from his parents. Twice a term he was allowed a weekend at home so he could see for himself what was going on.

Other children had it just as hard but because of different circumstances. By now Terry Heather from Dagenham was staying with his third family as an evacuee in Somerset. This time he was on a farm. He felt that the family did not have much faith in his level of cleanliness because he was forced to wash in a bowl outside the house. The farmer was responsible for two German prisoners of war who worked

The dangers of smoking were not known during the war as this advertisement shows. Cigarettes were often presented as gifts to members of the forces.

The Forces' Favourite

Player's Please

MEDIUM OR MILD · PLAIN OR CORK TIPS

for him. He also invited them home for tea on a Sunday. Terry remembers that they both seemed quite happy with their situation. Although Terry received a number of letters from home he did not have much idea of what was going on back in Essex. He was more concerned with what was happening in the town he was living in. It was now home to youngsters who had been sent to the country from parts of London as well as Essex. The evacuees went to Somerset schools and mixed with local children. The teachers were also a mix of locals and those from evacuation areas – Terry remembers some from his old school and others he did not know.

Local press reports of air raids still could not name the exact locations of attacks. In Essex-based newspapers the raids were described as having taken place 'within the South East District'. There were no specific casualty numbers given either. All reporters could say was that a 'large number of buildings' had been damaged resulting in 'numerous casualties'. However, one report in the *Romford Times* in early 1941 was more specific. It described a blitz on South Street, but it did include the words 'only now can we report this', so there was no way for readers to tell when the raid actually occurred. In fact, the bombs had fallen on 9 December.

It was not only the position of air raids that newspapers were ordered to keep secret. Photographs of children who were being evacuated from Essex were often printed, but captions never stated where they had been evacuated to.

Everyone who lived through the war has a story to tell about the air raids. John Smith remembers walking home from the cinema in Romford at about 9 p.m. and as he turned into Como Street an enemy plane dropped a bomb. He ran down an

The Dagenham Girl Pipers performed numerous shows for the troops. This one was an official engagement for the Ministry of Information. *(Dagenham Girl Pipers)*

Badges of the Essex air-raid warden service. Full uniform was a sign of an effective warden.

alley at the back of the shops in North Street and threw himself to the ground. After a few minutes he got up and started to walk home again. Another bomb was dropped, but instead of falling to the ground where he stood, John ran back to the spot in the alley where he had lain down before. When he got home the rest of the family was in the Anderson shelter in the garden. John's mother was very glad to see him but then told him off for going to the cinema. The bombs had fallen on Marks Road. When John told everyone about running back to the alley he was subjected to a lot of leg-pulling.

In September there were changes in the rules governing how wardens should act during raids. In the past whistles had been blown to supplement public sirens, but this was now only to happen if a large number of incendiaries fell in the immediate area. Warden patrols were also supposed to be limited to times of public alerts, but often raids occurred when no alert had been given.

Wardens were also required to find out where residents went to shelter during a raid. A report from Southend Air Raid Precautions Department explained how when a row of nine houses was completely demolished by bombs, the wardens knew which public shelters the occupants went to and whether they used Anderson shelters. This knowledge made it possible to find out which houses had been empty by checking the shelters for their inhabitants and saved time that might previously have been spent looking for possible casualties.

Although not yet due for call-up, Joan Francis of Thorpe-le-Soken volunteered to join the RAF in 1941. This was what every girl wanted to do because of the attractive uniforms issued by the service, she said. Joan was turned down and joined the Land Army instead. She was interviewed at home by the Essex Land Army welfare superintendent who took girls into her own home for training. Joan's duties included mucking out bullock pens, collecting eggs, making butter and learning how to pluck turkeys.

Joining the Land Army gave Joan the opportunity to meet other girls from very different backgrounds, a common effect of wartime service. Her room-mates included a very elegant girl who worked with embroidery at Harrods and another who was the eldest of thirteen children from the East End of London. Joan suffered from an infected heel, which took some time to recover as there were no antibiotics then.

When the other girls left after six weeks' training, Joan was forced to stay behind because of her injury. Her brother, who was in the army by then, walked 5 miles from Harwich to visit her while he was on embarkation leave. The household staff would not let him into Joan's bedroom until she could convince them that he was her brother.

In May a Civic Restaurant opened in Tilbury. Civic Restaurants were being set up throughout the county – Dagenham already had three – and they were supplied by emergency food vans presented to the borough by the Ford Motor Company. They served cheap meals that were not restricted by rationing. Some of these establishments were still in existence many years after the war. The one at Wantz Hall in Dagenham survived into the early 1960s, providing reasonably priced food for pensioners, and even for schoolchildren during the holidays.

In addition to entertaining the troops, the Dagenham Girl Pipers also carried out war work. These three members are piped back from their work in the fields as Land Girls. *(Dagenham Girl Pipers)*

As well as delivering to restaurants, mobile food vans also provided meals to schools, docks, farms and factories. In addition, there were mobile canteens that would arrive quickly at bomb sites to offer refreshment to those whose homes were damaged and the emergency services who were on site to help them.

Business had to continue in spite of the war. Advertisements in the local press tried to persuade members of the public to change the ration-providing shop with which they were registered. The Co-op launched a campaign to get customers to re-register at one of its branches. It promised that all Co-op shoppers would get their full quota of rations and that they would get a fair share of unrationed food too.

The production of many goods was suspended for the war period so that effort could be concentrated on making urgent supplies. The manufacture of permitted goods, for example furniture and clothing, had to be based on the Utility style, which did not require as much material or skill as pre-war designs.

At the beginning of the war the building of buses was suspended, but it soon became clear that more vehicles were needed to transport workers to factories, and so production was started again in the form of the little-known 'Utility bus'. The vehicle was designed under the auspices of the Ministry of Supply and the Ministry of War Transport. The aim of the engineers was to reduce the quantity of materials and the level of skill needed to make a bus. Some companies, such as Ford at Dagenham, had already shown the way forward and had managed to change the production process so that it could be run by semi-skilled operatives without the need for highly skilled men. These methods were applied to bus manufacture. All rounded parts of the bodywork were removed, giving the vehicle, a Bristol K5G, a very angular appearance. Later models had wooden seats with no upholstery. Even the size of tickets was reduced to save paper.

Local councils in Essex began a 'Justice for Essex Campaign' in 1941. They attempted to force the government to help them cope with falling levels of rates which resulted from the loss of local people who were evacuated or serving in the forces and those who had moved because their homes had been bombed.

Further improvements were made to Beacon Hill Fort in Harwich when a Cornwallis Battery was added. Consisting of twin 6-pounder guns and five pillboxes, it was intended to provide ground defence in the event of an attack by enemy troops.

A Noak Hill woman, Mrs Hollick of Dacre Cottages, Paternoster Row, got a nasty shock when someone knocked on her door at 5.30 one morning. The visitor turned out to be a German airman, the only survivor of a Dornier bomber shot down by the RAF. He was wounded and she helped him on to the sofa. It turned out that his plane had crashed in Harts Wood, Brentwood. Mrs Hollick had two sons who were both serving in the army and one of them was home on leave. He questioned the airman while Mr Hollick called the police and went to find the parachute.

Name...

No..................................

You are now a member of the Women's Land Army.
You are pledged to hold yourself available for
     service on the land for the period of the war.
You have promised to abide by the conditions of
     training and employment of the Women's
     Land Army; its good name is in your hands.
You have made the home fields your battlefield.
     Your country relies on your loyalty and
     welcomes your help.

Signed...
                                        Honarary Director
Signed...
                                        Committee Chairman
Date.............................

I realise the national importance of the work
     which I have undertaken and I will serve
     well and faithfully.

Signed...

The enrolment form for the Women's Land Army.

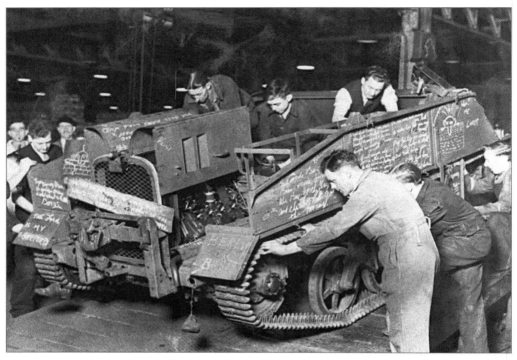

The Ford Motor Company transferred production from civilian to military vehicles during the war. Its systems meant that semi-skilled employees could manufacture products without the need for support from many skilled workers. *(Ford Motor Company)*

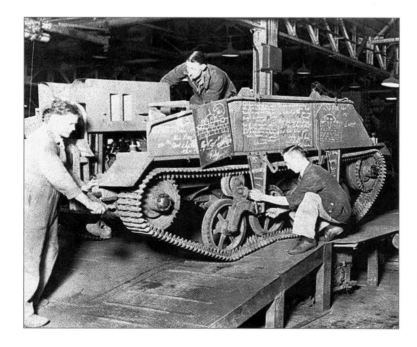

The vehicle under production has several messages to the enemy chalked on its sides. *(Ford Motor Company)*

Clothes rationing was introduced in June 1941. Everyone was issued with sixty-six coupons a year. Shops now had to label clothes to show their coupon value as well as their price. Later in the year more items were added to the list of rationed foodstuffs, including canned meat and fish. Rationing was not always enforced fairly. A Romford butcher was charged with supplying meat to a customer without coupons. The authorities were obviously very keen to be seen to deal with such cases severely because he was fined £100, a colossal amount for the time. The customer fared even worse: he was sent to prison.

Other items were in short supply and this led to self-imposed rationing. The shortage of paper meant that newspapers were not able to print as many copies as they would have liked. The *Stratford Express* started an appeal for copies to be passed on to members of the armed forces after they had been read by the public. There was even a shortage of alarm clocks, which made life difficult for those who had to get up early. Shortages had an adverse effect on many shops which were forced to close because of a lack of stock.

There were many examples of rationing not working to everyone's satisfaction. Romford residents were resigned to putting up with people from Hornchurch, Rainham and other local areas coming to their market to buy food. However, they drew the line at 'foreigners' who flooded the town on market days, buying up what was available. The foreigners in question were actually the residents of nearby Dagenham.

Many servicemen based at Essex military establishments were from, or would later join, the ranks of celebrities. Some future stars began their careers during the war in organisations like ENSA (the Entertainments National Service Association). It was not only the troops who were entertained by the concert parties; they also did performances for factory workers, usually in the canteen at lunchtime.

ENSA was the beginning of a career in showbusiness for some, but others who were later to become household names took a different route to the stage. One of them was Max Bygraves. He was an airman at Hornchurch Aerodrome and he spent his free evenings performing at local pubs, including the Elm Park Hotel and the Beacon in Dagenham. (He met his wife at the base and admitted that he did most of his courting in Romford.)

There were a large number of sportsmen in the forces. Some spent their time in the services playing football or cricket for military teams, but by no means all. The Essex cricketer Kenneth Parsons was killed in action.

News of those fighting on all fronts was reported in Essex's newspapers. Martin Jones of Manor Road, Romford, was awarded the Distinguished Service Medal (DSM) when he was still only nineteen. He was serving on a British submarine – of course the paper that carried the news could not name the vessel or give any details about the nature or location of incident in which Jones displayed such bravery. Elsewhere, the newspapers announced that Mrs Ethel Batterham of Stanway had heard that her husband, who had been reported missing, was now a prisoner of war.

Heroes of the Home Front featured in more detailed reports. John Grayston, an engineer, and Bert Vincent, a foreman, worked at Romford Gas Works. They were

This poster urged the population to 'Go Forward Together'. While the majority may have taken its advice, there were still some who didn't.

both awarded the George Medal when they risked their lives to turn off the gas supply to pipes that had been fractured during an air raid and were on fire. Although details of the incident were printed, this story was reported long after it happened.

Some members of the home front defence forces were mentioned in the press for different, often tragic, reasons. After attending a dance, a 27-year-old Home Guard corporal was shot and died. Whether it was an accident or suicide is not known. The man had tried to join the army but was declared unfit. His father reported that he slept with a gun under his pillow.

In 1941 there was a change to the regulations covering civil defence workers which stated that anyone employed as a full-time air-raid warden could not leave the service without the officer-in-charge's permission. It also became an offence for any warden to disobey an order or be absent without permission. The punishment for these offences was a £10 fine or a month in prison, or both.

The River Thames had been under attack from the first days of the war and a mine-watching system was set up and had been in place since 1939. Downriver from Dagenham sailing barges were moored every quarter of a mile. Each had three mine watchers on board. Anyone who had any business near the river was also enlisted to help in the constant search for mines. This included military personnel, members of the Home Guard and civilians. After an air raid a £5 reward was offered to anyone who spotted a mine that was subsequently destroyed by disposal experts.

Soldiers posted to Chelmsford were presented with a booklet called *Welcome To Essex* by the Essex War Welfare Committee. It included information about the town and its soldiers' clubs, among other things. Later editions were printed for sale to the public. The committee was also responsible for publishing *Battle over Essex* at the end of the war.

In April there was a rise in the number of incendiaries dropped on Romford. The raids of the 19th and 20th claimed 25 per cent of the total number of fatal casualties to occur in the town during the whole war: thirty-five people died. In June over forty people were killed in one raid on Essex Road. The figure included several children.

A tea break for the Dagenham Girl Pipers while entertaining the troops at a YMCA. *(Dagenham Girl Pipers)*

COUNTY BOROUGH OF SOUTHEND - ON - SEA.

AIR RAID PRECAUTIONS DEPARTMENT.

Ref:- Y/S.

Circ. No. 455.

120, Victoria Avenue,

Southend-on-Sea.

30th April 1941.

To:-

Whole-time Air Raid Wardens.

REGULATION 29B OF THE DEFENCE (GENERAL) REGULATIONS 1939.

THE CIVIL DEFENCE (EMPLOYMENT & OFFENCES) ORDER 1941.

Under the provisions of the above mentioned Regulation and Order any person who is employed whole-time as an Air Raid Warden is required to continue in his/her employment until his/her services are dispensed with by the Officer in charge of the Service to which he/she belongs, whether his/her services are dispensed with at his/her own desire or otherwise.

Under the same Regulation and Order if any person employed whole-time as an Air Raid Warden (a) disobeys any lawful order given to him/her in the course of that employment, or (b) without reasonable excuse is absent from any place at a time when it is his/her duty to be there in the course of that employment he/she will be guilty of an offence, and will, on summary conviction, be liable to imprisonment for a term of not exceeding one month or to a fine not exceeding £10, or to both such imprisonment and such fine.

It would be a matter of deep regret to me to think that the discipline and efficiency of the Service depended upon penal sanctions, and I confidently believe that although this is a young Service it has acquired an esprit de corps comparable with H. M. Fighting Forces.

Air Raid Precautions Officer.

By 1941 regulations for civil defence groups were being enforced with stronger sanctions. It seems that some had to be forced into doing their duty.

The public was continually warned not to touch strange objects found lying on the ground. A Ministry of Information announcement reminded people that collecting souvenirs was illegal. It reported how one man tried to knock the contents out of an incendiary device by banging it on a plough: it blew up.

The year 1941 saw the arrival of prisoners of war in the county. These men were mainly Italian. A camp was built for them on Wakering Common. Many were given a great deal of freedom and were employed on local farms.

Prisoners of war were not the only new workers arriving in Essex at this time. Chelmsford had three large factories which needed staff, and many of the new employees were transferred to the town from other parts of the country.

In June the decision was taken to manufacture machine guns in Britain. Previously, the guns had been bought from the United States, but money had now run out and the army was very short of weapons. The contract to produce them was awarded to a Dagenham factory – an unusual move given that the company had never made weapons before. However, just as men were conscripted into the army, factories were conscripted into war work to produce what the government told them to. The Sterling Refrigerator Company made 50,000 guns based on the design of a German Schmeisser. These weapons were known as Lancasters after the man who designed them.

The 5th Essex Battalion Home Guard, covering Brentwood and Ingatestone, was issued with an 'Invasion Booklet'. It was marked 'not to be handed to the public'. It answered what were described as vital questions, such as how can the enemy land airborne troops and could this be done at night? The booklet said it was unlikely that an airborne invasion would be capable of taking over the garrisons in Britain. It also said it was probable that single German parachutists were already landing to send back information by wireless. The duty of the Home Guard was to hasten the completion of defences, train hard and be constantly ready for invasion.

In July tests were begun on large guns at Shoebury. Earlier in the war the Germans had fired huge railway-based guns that were capable of reaching across the Channel into Kent. There were several attempts to create a gun that could return the compliment.

By the end of the year the total personnel at Hornchurch Aerodrome consisted of 78 officers, 1,269 airmen, 314 airwomen, 6 platoons of the Essex Regiment, a detachment of Royal Artillery, a Canadian anti-aircraft battery and some members of the Royal Tank Corps. The Canadians were just one of the many international units who served at the base. There were also pilots from Czechoslovakia, France, Australia and New Zealand.

While many foreigners were in Britain aiding the war effort, the people of Essex tried to assist those abroad. In December there was a 'Help for Russia Week'. Toys and books were collected for Russian children who were suffering during the German invasion.

There were several fund-raising activities in Essex in 1941. A war weapons week in Colchester was very successful, so much so that the balance of the money raised after paying for weapons was enough to meet the cost of a servicemen's hostel in

Several older defences around the Essex coast were brought back into use during the Second World War. Point Clear Martello tower was built in 1805 to repel invasion from Napoleonic France. During the war modern guns were mounted on the roof and it was used as a lookout post. The Martello tower is now a museum. *(East Essex Aviation Museum)*

The view from the top of Point Clear Martello tower across the Colne and Blackwater Estuaries. *(East Essex Aviation Museum)*

the town. Other plans were introduced by the government to raise money for the war, among them an increase in taxes on luxuries. Duty on cigarettes had risen from 1s on a packet of twenty to 1s 6d by December.

By the end of 1941 conscription had been expanded to include unmarried women up to the age of thirty. They were offered the choice of joining the auxiliary services or taking a job in industry. The age of those excused service because they were in a reserved occupation was raised, and married men could now be directed away from their families to work in other areas.

Service in the Civil Defence and Home Guard also became compulsory. This upset many of those who had volunteered and some resigned. This was no more than a gesture, however, because they were immediately directed to re-enlist.

There was a new appeal to the people of Colchester to take strangers into their homes, this time old people from evacuation areas. Householders were offered 5s a head and neighbours were encouraged to work together to accept lodgers so that the elderly people would not be lonely but would have someone they knew close by. At a Colchester Council meeting the question was raised as to why the town was being asked to take these evacuees when it was itself designated an evacuation area.

New crimes specific to the conditions placed on daily life during the war were now being committed. A clerk at Day's Transport of Priory Street, Colchester, was charged with selling petrol coupons. He received a year's probation. A woman from Wix was summonsed at Mistley for a rare offence. She had written to a friend in Ireland and asked her to send some bacon for Christmas. Her letter was intercepted by the Post Office and photographed. It was stated in court that anyone in Ireland was allowed to send food to England if they wanted to. However, it was against the law for anyone in Britain to ask someone in Ireland to send supplies. The woman was fined £1.

Needless to say, reports of crimes unrelated to the war continued, among both military personnel and civilians. A seventeen-year-old private from the Essex Regiment was charged with stealing 10s from one of his comrades. His sergeant major said the boy was of no use to his country at all. He was not only a thief but was also a bad influence on the rest of his regiment. He went on to say that the army did not want the teenager back. It turned out that they did, however – he was also a deserter and was taken away by a military escort.

In December an article by the Bishop of Chelmsford was published in the *Daily Mail*. He criticised the idea of ringing church bells as a warning in the event of an invasion. The bishop suggested that it would be better for the Home Guard to set off warning rockets. He asked exactly who was going to ring the bells, the German parachutists? He also suggested that in the event of invasion, soft soap should be spread over road junctions to make it difficult for German vehicles to make progress.

FIVE

1942: New Allies and New Enemies

By 1942 the main focus of the war had moved away from Europe to the Far East and Russia. As a result, things were a little quieter at home, but the atmosphere was enlivened by the arrival of the Americans in Britain when the United States entered the war after the attack on Pearl Harbor.

The more aggressive actions of the Japanese led to some Australian troops being redeployed from the battle in Libya. This gave the Germans a chance to make inroads into Allied positions. The loss of airfields made it more difficult to support Malta and the garrison on the island came under concerted German attack.

In the Atlantic in February the Germans launched their new U-boat supply ships, which made it possible for submarines to take on food and other essentials at sea. This led to more success against Allied shipping despite a bigger push against the German Navy by more ships and longer-range aircraft.

February also saw the surrender of Malaya to a Japanese force that was half the strength of the Allied defenders. It was one of Britain's worst defeats and it threatened the premiership of Winston Churchill.

In March the Lancaster bomber came into service with the RAF, and Arthur (Bomber) Harris, the new leader of Bomber Command, implemented his policy of heavy attacks on German cities. Also in this month the mass extermination of Jews began at Auschwitz in Poland.

In April there were discussions between the Special Operations Executive (SOE), a subversive group set up by Churchill, and MI6 concerning plans to assassinate both Hitler and Mussolini. May saw the resupply of Malta and the arrival of a number of new Spitfires on the island, delivered in a joint Anglo-American operation using aircraft carriers.

In June Tobruk fell to the Germans and the Allied forces had to retreat into Egypt; by July the enemy forces, led by Rommel, had reached El Alamein. A month later Churchill was in Egypt visiting the Eighth Army. October saw the attack at El Alamein that at last gave the Allies the victory they had been praying for. By early November Allied forces were back in Tobruk.

In August electronic devices became important in the conflict. There had been improvements in the use of radar as a tool for finding U-boats, but the Germans matched Allied progress by installing radar in their submarines. They could also jam the RAF's electronic bombing aid, known as GEE.

The widespread belief that everyone in the country was pulling together was not quite true. Theft of wood from damaged houses was quite common. In some cases inhabitants would return home to find window and door frames missing. Both made excellent firewood. Many of the perpetrators were identified and fined in court.

Crime increased during the war, especially among young people. The disruption to schools during hostilities seems to have led to a fall in literacy rates and a rise in delinquency. Youths even damaged equipment used for the protection of the public. For example, in Dagenham hooligans smashed fire service property.

There was also a rise in crime as a result of desertion from the army. Deserters could not get ration books and therefore had little option but to live outside the law, surviving by theft.

A woman at Boxford Petty Sessions was fined £2 for a war-related offence. She was a bus proprietor and had used one of her vehicles to take people to a darts match. She was charged with the misuse of petrol. A deputy chief warden in Romford was charged with the same offence after driving his wife to the dog track. His higher position must have influenced the level of his punishment because he was fined £20.

While some of the population were wasting fuel, the *Essex County Standard* was offering prizes to those who could conserve it. The newspaper invited competition entries for recipes that were quick, easy and economical to make. The winner was a savoury rice dish.

The shortage of food even affected perks for air-raid wardens. The supply of tea, milk and biscuits to warden posts was discontinued. However, there was a way round the restriction: wardens could use some of their subsistence allowance, which was introduced for part-timers, to buy tea from group centre canteens. The allowance was 9*d* for those who worked between two and four hours, 1*s* 6*d* for between four and eight hours, and 3*s* for between eight and twelve hours. In Southend the tea problem was solved when the air-raid precautions officer was allowed by the Ministry of Food to buy tea and other goods and then resell them to the warden posts.

The hostilities had a great effect on family life in a number of ways. The suspension of house building meant that young couples setting out on married life were even more likely to be forced to live with their parents than before the war. If they were lucky enough to be able to set up a home, they could get vouchers for furniture – a choice of light or dark oak. Among young couples who did have their own home, husbands were usually off fighting so single-parent families were the norm. Extended families were also often forced to live together because of bomb damage to houses.

Rationing began to bite everyone, even preventing wardens having a cup of tea at their posts when they were on duty. It took an agreement with the Ministry of Food to overcome this problem.

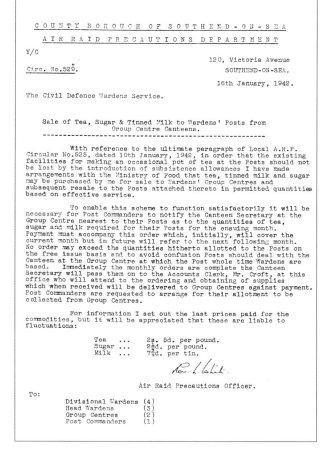

COUNTY BOROUGH OF SOUTHEND-ON-SEA

AIR RAID PRECAUTIONS DEPARTMENT

Y/C
                                                    120, Victoria Avenue
Circ. No.529.   SOUTHEND-ON-SEA.

                                                    16th January, 1942.

The Civil Defence Wardens Service.

        Sale of Tea, Sugar & Tinned Milk to Wardens' Posts from
                         Group Centre Canteens.

        With reference to the ultimate paragraph of Local A.R.P.
Circular No.525, dated 10th January, 1942, in order that the existing
facilities for making an occasional pot of tea at the Posts should not
be lost by the introduction of subsistence allowances I have made
arrangements with the Ministry of Food that tea, tinned milk and sugar
may be purchased by me for sale to Wardens' Group Centres and
subsequent resale to the Posts attached thereto in permitted quantities
based on effective service.

        To enable this scheme to function satisfactorily it will be
necessary for Post Commanders to notify the Canteen Secretary at the
Group Centre nearest to their Posts as to the quantities of tea,
sugar and milk required for their Posts for the ensuing month.
Payment must accompany this order which, initially, will cover the
current month but in future will refer to the next following month.
No order may exceed the quantities hitherto allotted to the Posts on
the free issue basis and to avoid confusion Posts should deal with the
Canteen at the Group Centre at which the Post whole time Wardens are
based. Immediately the monthly orders are complete the Canteen
Secretary will pass them on to the Accounts Clerk, Mr. Croft, at this
office who will attend to the ordering and obtaining of supplies
which when received will be delivered to Group Centres against payment.
Post Commanders are requested to arrange for their allotment to be
collected from Group Centres.

        For information I set out the last prices paid for the
commodities, but it will be appreciated that these are liable to
fluctuations:

                Tea   ...   2s. 5d. per pound.
                Sugar ...   2½d. per pound.
                Milk ...   7¾d. per tin.

                        Air Raid Precautions Officer.
        To:
                Divisional Wardens (4)
                Head Wardens   (3)
                Group Centres   (2)
                Post Commanders   (1)

Young girls had to do either active service or work in munitions factories. Teenagers then were no different to today's and often parents would come home to find that, on account of a healthy young appetite, a teenager had eaten a week's supply of rations.

It wasn't just homes that were in danger of being damaged in air raids: there was also disruption to and destruction of local services. Even if a family's house was not bombed, gas and electricity supplies might be cut off because of damage elsewhere. This would often disrupt routine: during the war years many households kept to the strict practice of wash day on Monday and ironing day on Tuesday. The enforced change to this small part of normal life would have been more widespread were it not for the fact that most laundry was still done by hand and water was often heated using solid fuel boilers.

The breakdown in the fabric of life was noticeable in the condition of Essex's roads. The County Council admitted that road surfaces were deteriorating not only because of bomb damage but also as a result of normal wear and tear. A lack of building materials meant that only emergency repairs could be carried out.

Ebenlowelle Walker was far from Dagenham in 1942 and was now a soldier serving in Egypt with the Royal Army Service Corps (RASC). He also spent some time as a POW. *(Sylvia Walker)*

Disruption to any public service caused stress for the population but this was especially true of the Post Office. A person whose loved ones were away fighting would dread the arrival of the postman, fearing the delivery of a telegram. But the postman was also the source of comforting news, letters from far away providing reassurance that servicemen were still alive and well.

The problems suffered by families at home are often forgotten in the history of the armed conflict. A Guild was formed on Dagenham's Becontree Estate for the families of prisoners of war. Members held regular monthly meetings, getting together with others who were in the same situation to obtain information about

Ebenlowelle Walker in a truck in the desert. *(Sylvia Walker)*

procedures for contacting loved ones. The Red Cross produced a monthly magazine called *The Prisoner of War* which was free to the families.

No doubt some members of the Guild had the same problems as the wives of other men in the forces: women complained about the low rates of service allowance paid to them. Although Dagenham bordered London, it was part of Essex. Women in the capital with husbands in the forces received 3s 6d a week more in allowances than those in rural areas, which is how Essex was rated.

In Colchester a prisoner-of-war flag day raised £400. A dance at the officers' club in the town raised £100 for the same cause. The music was provided by the band of the Royal Berkshire Regiment. At this time over 200 men from the town were in enemy captivity. Each received a weekly food parcel to the value of 10s.

The story of one prisoner of war was printed in the *Essex County Standard*. Frank English of the Royal Tank Regiment told how he and some other soldiers stopped a convoy of armoured cars in the western desert of Libya. It turned out that the vehicles were being driven by Germans. Frank and his mates were captured. After five days' captivity he braved a minefield to escape.

The Ford Motor Company of Dagenham provided a number of emergency food vans to local councils. Romford was given two in February. The vehicles were mobile canteens that could quickly bring refreshments to both emergency service workers and victims of enemy attack.

A novel form of defence for the Thames Estuary was built in Northfleet by Holloway Brothers. The Maunsell Forts were constructed at the company's yard before being towed into position. There were three army forts and one for the navy. Each had seven towers connected by walkways. They gave early warning of air attacks and were also armed with anti-aircraft guns.

Another attempt to collect scrap metal was put into operation in 1942. There was a similar drive to save waste paper. If there was one thing Essex did well during the war, it was collecting for recycling, although it is debatable how much effect this had on the war effort.

Raising money to pay for arms and equipment remained a feature of life on the home front. The town of Barking adopted a destroyer in March. The *Undaunted* was under construction at the time and went on to take part in the Normandy landings in June 1944.

Cases of suicide resulting from fear of the war were still not uncommon, but a young man from Dagenham killed himself at this time for a different reason. He was refused entry to the army because he suffered from asthma. He already had three brothers in the services and could not stand the shame of not being allowed to join them.

The manning of some anti-aircraft guns was transferred to the Home Guard at this stage of the war. Many of the small army units manning these positions were often in such secluded places that they had little idea what was happening in other areas.

Because the number of air raids had decreased, in 1942 Sylvia Walker and her family returned to Dagenham from their evacuation homes in Swindon. The raids had not stopped completely, however. If enemy aircraft came over while she was at Roding School, Sylvia and the other children had to lie down in the cloakroom because they had no shelters to go to. All the children had a biscuit put on their chest and they would sing 'Nick Nack Paddy Whack' and 'Ten Green Bottles' to take their minds off the raid. When there were night-time attacks the family would go to the shelter in the garden and wait until it was over before going to bed. The local warden would come round and shout down to check whether everyone was all right. The neighbours would also keep an eye on the family because Sylvia's mother was on her own with five children while her father was fighting in Egypt.

The war was not entirely full of bad experiences for the RASC in Egypt. Here Ebenlowelle Walker and some of his friends are visiting the pyramids. *(Sylvia Walker)*

Ebenlowelle Walker (right) named one of his lorries Gert after his wife Gertrude. *(Sylvia Walker)*

After raids, children would go out in the morning to gather shrapnel, competing to find the biggest piece. They all went to look at the damage and played on bomb sites. The death and destruction did not really affect them.

One bomb fell on a house at Martin's Corner, Dagenham, where a wedding celebration was taking place. The bride, the groom and all the guests were killed. Dr Stewart's surgery near Bennetts Castle Lane was also bombed. The explosion jammed the front door of the Walker family's house for some time. When they got out, they went to the bomb site to get firewood and to search for any unbroken windows to replace their own which had been smashed.

Sylvia Walker had some close calls. During one raid while on the way to the shelter she saw red balls of fire coming from the planes and as she looked up at them she fell into the garden pond. On another occasion she was at her friend's house when a raid began. She ran home but on the way a plane swooped low. She threw herself to the ground and watched as it went past. It was so low that it skimmed the roof of a house and knocked its chimney down.

One of Sylvia's brothers also had a close encounter with a German aircraft. While walking home from school he saw a German bomber being chased by a Spitfire. Both were flying very low. The German plane dropped a bomb on Erkenwald School's playing field. It bounced and went through a row of houses without exploding. Sylvia's brother collected bullets and shells which had fallen from aircraft

Ebenlowelle Walker was not the only person from Dagenham to spend part of the war in Egypt. The Girl Pipers went there to entertain the troops. (Dagenham Girl Pipers)

and hid them in the Walkers' back garden. When he returned to them they were gone; someone had stolen them.

There were still serious fears of invasion and by now Canadian artillery had been placed all around the outskirts of Colchester. At the end of April it looked as though invasion could become a reality when the Canadian gunners were called back on duty by messages flashed across cinema screens.

Early in the year one of the lesser-known airfields of Essex began operation: RAF Bradwell Bay. Information was withheld about this site because it deployed radar, still a well-kept secret even after the war. The base was situated at Bradwell-juxta-Mare, just beyond Southminster. One of the first squadrons to fly from there used Canadian Boston light bombers.

The common wartime image of Land Girls is of young women working on farms in the countryside. This was not always the case. Joan Francis from Thorpe-le-Soken was sent to her permanent Land Girl position at the sports ground owned by London match manufacturers Bryant & May. Ray Park was in Snakes Lane, Woodford. Most of the ground had been ploughed up and the girls grew onions, carrots and cabbages. There was also a poultry area which was later changed to rabbit production. Some parts of the sports ground survived, such as the putting green, tennis courts and showers, which the girls could use. There were five Land Girls at the site – three locals, Joan and another import. Joan and the other girl lived

Land Army girls at Ray Park, the Bryant & May match factory sports ground in Snakes Lane, Woodford. Joan Francis is at the back on the right. *(Joan Francis)*

As well as digging for victory, the neighbours were advised to join together and form a pig club. They could feed the animal scraps from their kitchens and then share out the meat when it was slaughtered.

in the manager's house. There were also four men, one of whom drove an ancient tractor. In addition to vegetables and livestock, there was also a walled garden where fruit was grown. Joan believes that the fruit went to the Bryant & May factory for the board of governors. At Ray Park the workers were able to watch the bombing of London from a safe distance.

Joan's sister was now seventeen and used to borrow a Land Army uniform so that she could accompany Joan and her friends to dances held at Abridge Aerodrome. These were weekly events and were held for the air force and army personnel from numerous Allied countries who were stationed there.

The Dig for Victory campaign was now well under way and every open space was turned over to growing vegetables. Unlike Ray Park, not all land was willingly given up, however. Church property in Doddinghurst Road, Brentwood, had to be requisitioned by the ARP on which to grow vegetables.

Despite Colchester's obvious military targets, over the course of the war the town escaped with relatively light enemy action. Nevertheless, there were some serious raids.

When Severalls Mental Hospital was bombed in August thirty-eight people were killed. Photographs of the damage were published in the local press but, of course, the newspapers did not name the area where the attack occurred.

It was lucky that many of the children from Barking Abbey School had been evacuated because the building was severely damaged by bombing in June. Not all children were evacuated from the area, however, and several mothers kept young ones at home with them. While the women were employed doing important war work, some of their children were cared for in nurseries, including those opened in Barking at Eastbury Manor House and at Lodge Farm House.

The fact that not everyone, for whatever reason, was prepared to fight in the war was recognised and accepted by the authorities. Conscientious objectors were excused military service if they undertook other war work, such as civil defence duties. Many ended up working on farms in Essex. One man, however, refused to do either agricultural or civil defence tasks because he was a Jehovah's Witness.

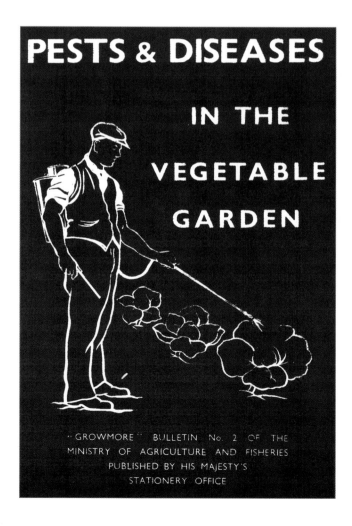

The government produced a number of booklets and leaflets, such as this pests and diseases pamphlet, to help the novice gardener produce crops as part of the Dig for Victory campaign.

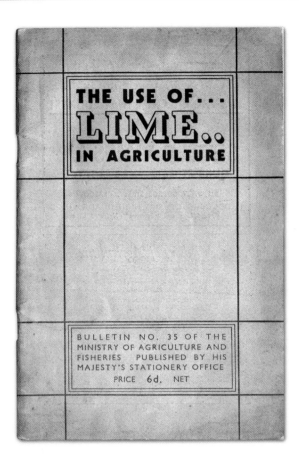

This booklet explains the advantages of the use of lime in gardening.

In 1942 he was sent to prison for three months. A man from Hornchurch was sentenced to three months in prison for refusing to do land work instead of joining the forces. It turned out that he had already served six months for the same offence. He refused to do anything at all that was concerned with the war.

Some people could not wait to join the forces. Jimmy Underwood from Dagenham had tried to join the navy at fourteen. He was sent away. He tried again at fifteen and this time he was given a form that had to be signed by his parents to show they gave their permission. Jimmy finally convinced his parents to agree to his wishes and took the form back to the recruiting office in London Road, Romford. He was given a medical and passed as A1 but was sent away again until his sixteenth birthday. Then the navy called him back.

He did his training at Bristol and Portsmouth, which were both land bases. He then went to Scapa Flow to join his ship, the heavy cruiser HMS *Nigeria*. The vessel spent much of the early part of the year accompanying Russian convoys. Then in August the *Nigeria* became part of a supply convoy to Malta. During this mission the *Nigeria* was torpedoed and dive-bombed. She put into Gibraltar for repairs but then went to America for a refit.

While he was aboard Jimmy had little idea of what was going on at home. Other ships brought mail but deliveries were rare and the letters that did arrive were censored. There were restrictions on what his family could write about events back in Essex. Censorship worked in the other direction too: Jimmy was not allowed to tell his family where he was or what he was doing.

Continual reports from all sources said morale among the population was good, but some incidents seem to disprove this. When the journalist Tom Driberg stood as an independent candidate in the parliamentary by-election at Maldon in June he overturned a Conservative majority of 8,000 to win by 6,000. This must have been partly the result of the electorate's reaction to the fall of Tobruk four days before polling day. Driberg blamed the Conservatives' defeat on profiteers haggling at home while troops abroad waited for munitions.

It was not only setbacks for the troops abroad that affected morale. Heavy bombing in other parts of the country led to bad feeling among local populations who came to believe that the authorities were not doing a good job. When Liverpool suffered heavy bombing, rumours began to circulate that the population had revolted and the city was under martial law. There was also the case of the *Daily Worker*, the Communist Party newspaper which was suppressed by the government for eighteen months. Why was suppression necessary if morale was so good?

There is no doubt that Winston Churchill did much to keep the country going by both his actions and his character. He would sometimes turn up for an unannounced visit and as word spread, crowds would turn out to cheer him, even in the worst hit areas.

In 1942 there were calls from many quarters for the formation of a second front in Europe to help take pressure off the Russians. One champion of this view was the writer Charles Ashleigh. Stanley Holmes, MP for Dovercourt, warned against rushing into such a huge step until the country was ready. He said the decision should be left to Churchill.

One of the major training exercises organised in the county during the Second World War took place at Maldon in July. Operation Walrus was a simulated attack and invasion by enemy troops. It was intended to be a test of the combined power of the military and civil defence. The exercise was sanctioned by the regional commander of the Eastern Civil Defence Region. It was far from successful and the umpire's report stated that there had been an almost complete lack of liaison between the military and the borough invasion committee.

Petrol for the civilian motorist was in very short supply by August. Because of this the Ford Motor Company published instructions on how to lay a car up for the duration of the war.

Restrictions on the use of vehicles made travel difficult. This was one of the reasons why local councils made plans for stay-at-home holidays. It was hoped that a choice of local events would discourage families from travelling to other areas. Romford ran a five-week programme of entertainment, which included dances, concerts, sports days, circuses and funfairs. A crowd of between 4,000 and 5,000 people turned up for the opening ceremony of the Holiday at Home scheme at

COUNTY BOROUGH OF SOUTHEND-ON-SEA.
CIVIL DEFENCE CASUALTY SERVICES.

I M P O R T A N T   YOUR CO-OPERATION IN BRINGING THE FOLLOWING TO
THE NOTICE OF THOSE CONCERNED IS REQUESTED.

1.   GUILDFORD ROAD.   A new First Aid Post, Gas Cleansing Station,
First Aid Party and Ambulance Depot, provided in the former
Whitbread's Bottling Stores (and adjacent premises), GUILDFORD ROAD,
Southend, will be brought into operation on MONDAY next DECEMBER 14th.
at 1400 hours.

2.   The Guildford Road premises replace the following which as from
Monday next December 14th. at the times stated will cease to be
operational and revert to a care and maintenance basis.

   (a)   BOURNEMOUTH PARK ROAD First Aid Post, Gas Cleansing Station,
           First Aid Party and Ambulance Depot,
           CLOSES 0900 hours 14.12.42.

   (b)   MUNICIPAL HEALTH CENTRE First Aid Post, Gas Cleansing Station,
           First Aid Party and Ambulance Depot, (Warrior Square),
           CLOSES 1400 hours 14.12.42.

3.   GUILDFORD ROAD TELEPHONE NUMBERS.

           F.A.Party and Ambulance Depot (operations room)   No.67073
           F.A. Post. No.2054.
ALL operational messages should ordinarily be transmitted over
67073, but as an alternative 2054 can be used if the former line
is "dead", not merely engaged.

4.   THE TRANSPORT STAFF OFFICER, MR.BASS, will, after 1400 hours on
14.12.42. have his office at Guildford Road, Telephone No. 67073.

5.   WALKING CASUALTIES.   As a general rule walking casualties should
be directed as follows :-

AREA	F.A.POST	TEL.NO.
(1) East of Thorpe Hall Ave., Thorpe Bay.	Caulfield Road F.A.P.	Shoebury (531) No. 249.
(2) Line - Hamlet Court Rd., West Rd. eastwards to Thorpe Hall Avenue.	Guildford Road F.A.P.	2054
(3) Line - Norfolk Ave., Recreation Ave.Cliffsea Grove,Highcliff Drive, eastwards to line Hamlet Court Rd.West Road.	Southend General Hospital	3383
(4) West of line Norfolk Ave., Recreation Ave.,Cliffsea Grove, Highcliff Drive.	West Leigh F.A.P.	78534

The addresses of wartime first-aid posts in Southend.

Raphael's Park. It was introduced from the bandstand by the mayor. Colchester also promoted the Holiday at Home campaign and encouraged the use of local theatres, growing food and cycle rides as a way of spending leisure time. It would seem that the scheme was successful because Eastern National Buses reported that fewer passengers travelled during holiday time than on a normal day. When planning leisure activities, Colchester Council said it was unsure whether local munitions workers would be allowed time off to participate.

The Holiday at Home scheme seemed much more sensible after a large group from the Romford area went to stay in a hotel on the south-west coast. The hotel was owned by a well-known family of bakers from Mawney Road, Romford. The party were on the beach when a group of low-flying planes approached. The holiday-makers thought they were British until the aircraft began to machine-gun the sands.

It seems that local councils put more effort into the Holiday at Home scheme than the national government. When Dagenham Council applied to the Ministry of Health for permission to repair and reopen Leys open-air swimming pool it was refused.

However, Dagenham Council was also responsible for strange decisions which seemed to hamper the war effort. It refused permission for the 11th Battalion City of London, Dagenham Home Guard, to use Valance and Central Parks for training purposes. The council parks section argued that so many of the town's green areas had been turned over to the Dig for Victory scheme that it would be unfair to deprive the public of what little they had left.

The war brought more of the Essex countryside under cultivation. This reversed a trend that had been emerging for some time. In a local press report a man wrote that before the war his village had shrunk from a population of 480 to less than 300 because of the decline in farming. As part of the 'Ploughing Up' campaign thousands of miles of ditches were dug to help drainage, and other poorly used areas of land were also brought back into agricultural use. Of the 7,000 acres of marshland around the River Blackwater, half were now drained and under the plough.

By June there were rumours that Colchester would be completely evacuated of civilian personnel to make way for American servicemen. Work had begun on aerodromes for US planes and 1942 marked the final harvest for many Essex farms before land was covered in concrete. Because Essex was relatively flat it became the site of twelve US airfields, eight for bombers and four for fighters. The British government supplied the materials to build the US bases. Rubble used as hardcore for the runways came from London buildings damaged by bombing.

Many American pilots flew for the RAF well before the USA became involved in the war, but when the Americans officially arrived, the first Eagle squadrons were based at North Weald and then at Southend. Earls Colne airbase opened in September 1942 and then the first American bombers began to fly from Essex. A second American base was constructed at Great Saling and named Andrewsfield. The first inkling the villagers of Great Saling had of the planned airfield was when the land was requisitioned. This was soon followed by the arrival of 800 American servicemen of the Engineer Aviation Battalion.

The RAF set up a mobile unit in the Vicarage Field to feed the Americans and the vicar went out to greet the newly arrived men. What had been a track for horses and carts between Saling and the site was turned into a road big enough to take the large lorries that would be arriving at the airfield. The men were initially accommodated in tents, and when huts were finally built the engineers did not benefit from them because they were sent away to build more airfields.

The airfield at Saling had a dramatic effect on the locality; it transformed the landscape from farmland to acres of concrete. The newly made road was closed to the public but the track it replaced had been the quickest route to Stebbing, which caused great inconvenience for the locals. The village became entirely surrounded by the airbase and military personnel outnumbered the local population by more than six to one. Although many local farmers lost some of their land, they did find a new market for their produce. The airfield also brought famous visitors to the area. Bob Hope and James Cagney both came to the base to entertain the men.

In Colchester it seemed that the newly arrived Americans had taken over the town. The American Red Cross came with the airmen and opened a club over Marks &

The colour bar that the US military brought with it from home was not something that was known in England. When the Dagenham Girl Pipers entertained the troops everyone was treated equally. *(Dagenham Girl Pipers)*

Spencer's in Culver Street and an officers' club at the corner of High Street and St Nicholas Street. There was also a separate club for black servicemen in Priory Street.

The arrival of US personnel was not without problems. Any young British men who were still living in the area were often very unhappy at the Americans' familiarity with local girls. This often led to violence.

Another difference between US and British forces was the blankets with which personnel were issued. The Americans had much better quality grey blankets which enterprising women could turn into smart coats, not something they would have done with British khaki.

Not only airfields but also army bases were constructed in Essex as American servicemen poured into the county. Many of those who came to the county from the United States never left.

There were complaints in several parts of Essex that air-raid warnings were given too late. In many cases men at work in factories were sent to shelters while their families at home received no warning at all. It seemed that the authorities were more concerned with protecting the workforce than the rest of the population.

Witham station was severely damaged by bombing in August but was repaired the same day. Because of restrictions on the press the raid was not reported until six months later.

In September a Stirling bomber returning from a mission crashed near Weeley railway station. Although most of the crew escaped, the rear gunner was trapped.

Love Harold.

JOHN   RALPH.

Harold Howey with some friends from the Queen's Own Cameron Highlanders in Belgium. Before joining up Harold had served in the Home Guard at Little Oakley where he lived. (Olive Cooper)

Harold Howey, Queen's Own Cameron Highlanders, India. (Olive Cooper)

Two of the crew went back to help him but the plane exploded, killing them. The rear gunner was later released safely.

Essex formed the subject of a radio broadcast called *Calling British Forces in India*. A topical script about the county was prepared. The programme also included several messages for Essex servicemen.

In October the Sterling factory in Dagenham began to make a new machine gun. This was more advanced than the Lancaster it had been producing to date and was based on a design by George Patchett. He had worked in Czechoslovakia before the war and was smuggled out with his French wife on the orders of Winston Churchill when the Germans invaded the country. He brought with him plans for the latest design in machine guns.

On 16 October there were thanksgiving services throughout Essex and across the country marking the RAF's triumph over the Luftwaffe in the Battle of Britain and the victory in Egypt. Church bells called people to worship for the first time since the war began. Services were not only held in churches. On the afternoon of the same day nearly 1,000 civil defence workers went to a ceremony at the Regal Cinema in Colchester, which was also attended by the mayor.

In Chelmsford an innovation that began in wartime persisted beyond the end of hostilities. Dinners were introduced in many of the town's schools. This made the lives of working mothers much easier and so helped the war effort.

As the number of men called up increased, their departure left gaps in essential services. Many of the newly enlisted men had been air-raid wardens. In Romford there was now a serious shortage of recruits, which meant that the remaining wardens had to work much longer hours.

The restrictions placed on the civilian working population were evident when a Rainham man was summonsed for leaving his job at Woolwich Arsenal without permission. The man argued that the job was too easy and did not match his skill level. He was ordered to return to his employment.

Sunday morning buses stopped running in many parts of rural Essex by order of the traffic commissioner in November and there were also compulsory restrictions on milk rounds to save manpower and petrol.

December was not a good month for river traffic. The barge *Bankside*, loaded with flour, was sunk by a mine off Maplin Sands, killing the captain. Two days after Christmas another barge, the *Gertrude May*, hit a mine off Clacton and sank. It was also carrying flour.

At the end of the year a new crime, not punishable during peacetime, was introduced. Young women from a Chelmsford factory had visited a medium who told them that their factory would be bombed. She was charged with publishing statements likely to cause alarm. It was claimed that her predictions had led to many workers taking time off to avoid bombs. The woman was fined £10.

A special scheme was run at Christmas by the *Essex County Standard* and the Colchester Rotary Club. Soldiers based in the town were invited to spend Christmas Day in local households. Because of rationing, the invitations were for after 3 p.m. so that the guests did not come to dinner.

SIX

1943: The Tide Begins to Turn

January 1943 saw the tide turn in the war in Russia. Soviet forces began an offensive at Stalingrad and the siege of Leningrad was finally lifted. Much of the Russians' success was due to their speedy defeat of non-German forces, including the Hungarians. This month also saw the first moves in the uprising in the Warsaw Ghetto.

Early preparations were now under way for the Allied invasion of Europe, which would eventually come in 1944. Rommel left Africa after falling ill, knowing that the war there was lost. However, Hitler refused to allow the German Army to follow its commander. By May the last German forces had been defeated and Allied attentions turned toward Italy.

In Europe Allied bombing was having the effect on German cities that the Luftwaffe had attempted to achieve in Britain, and in Yugoslavia the partisans under Tito were fighting the Germans with the support of SOE in the form of both men and supplies.

The Dig for Victory campaign was such a success that by 1943 over a million tons of vegetables were being grown in gardens and allotments. The abundant harvest led to a vegetable-based recipe that was called Woolton Pie after the Minister for Food, Lord Woolton.

In July the Allies invaded Sicily where they found many Italian soldiers who were only too willing to give up the fight. By early September the Italians had surrendered but there was still some resistance, especially during the landing at Salerno that month. In response to the capitulation the Luftwaffe attacked the Italian fleet and sunk some of its ships. On Corfu German and Italian forces, former allies, now began to fight each other, and most of the northern half of Italy was under German control.

In December Churchill and Roosevelt finally met Stalin in Tehran. They informed the Russian leader of the plan to invade France in 1944 and Stalin promised to fight the Japanese when the war in Europe was over.

In Essex the war took a new turn in 1943. It is often said that after 1942 the war stopped north of Cambridge. Essex was never entirely free of attack right up to 1945, but there was certainly some let-up in enemy action. Because of this the ranks of civil defence workers were allowed to dwindle slightly. In Romford some older men were replaced by younger part-timers. Many of those who were asked to leave the civil defence organisations were ex-servicemen and they were not happy at being replaced.

The Home Guard was also losing men. A member of the guard's anti-aircraft gun crew, Sergeant Cawcutt, left to join the navy. He was a popular NCO and his unit presented him with an inscribed wallet to mark his departure.

There may have been a reduction in the number of raids, but those that did happen were lethal. The *Romford Times* reported how hundreds of early-morning workers on their way to businesses on the East London outskirts witnessed a large raid when German planes machine-gunned and bombed the area.

Travel during raids must have been frightening, but even when there was no bombing it was made very unpleasant by overcrowding. The people of Mersea complained to the Ministry of War about the crush on local buses. The increased number of factories in the county made the movement of workers much more difficult. Mersea had become a dormitory for war workers from Colchester. During

A poster encouraging the women of Britain to come into the factories.

Olive Cooper and some Wren colleagues on parade. *(Olive Cooper)*

Olive Cooper and other Wrens in Ceylon. Olive is on the right, kneeling. *(Olive Cooper)*

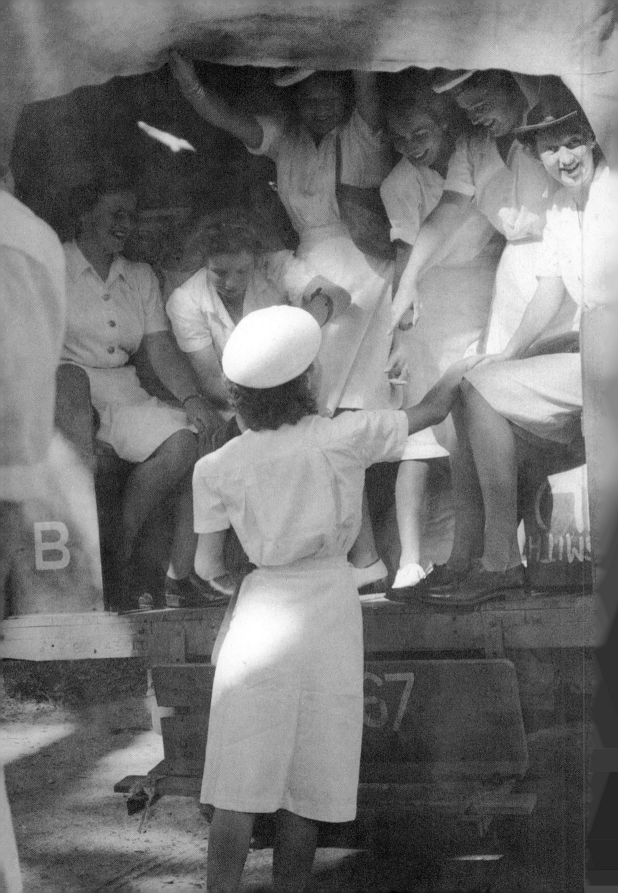

John Smith from Romford married his wife Olive at All Saints' church, Belvedere, two weeks before being sent to the Far East and the war against the Japanese. *(John Smith)*

rush hour the buses were terribly overcrowded because since peacetime there had been no rise in the number of vehicles in service. Workers were supposed to have priority, but it was reported that often many passengers who were just going shopping had seats while staff on their way to the factories had to stand.

It was not only enemy action that proved a threat to the population. Unexploded anti-aircraft shells were a great danger when they fell back to the ground. In Dagenham three men were killed by falling shells outside the Admiral Vernon public house in Broad Street.

Earlier in the war Olive Cooper had been working in the Co-op in Dovercourt, but she now enlisted in the WRNS (Wrens) and was posted to London. Although she kept in contact with her mother by letter, she had little idea of what was happening at home. She was so busy, however, that she barely had time to think about it. What she missed most was living by the seaside.

John Smith from Romford also enlisted. He joined the RAF Regiment, which had been formed early in the war. He was stationed at various places in England and

Opposite: Olive Cooper and friends on a truck in India. *(Olive Cooper)*

John and Olive Smith. The woman on the left is John's sister, the man on the right John's stepbrother who was his substitute best man. The original best man was in the army and had been sent overseas – a common problem for those planning wartime weddings. *(John Smith)*

Scotland before being posted abroad. While still in Britain he found out what was going on at home from the radio and newspapers. He also had some leave at home and heard news from other men coming back from leave in Essex. John married his wife Olive before he left UK shores and was then posted to the Far East with an armoured car and tank squadron. When he was overseas John thought of home all the time. He missed Romford but most of all he missed Olive. John says memories of the good times at home in Romford with family and friends kept him going through the hard times he spent in Burma.

Serious preparations for the D-Day landings were now under way. Barking Creek was the site of the manufacture of the Mulberry harbours to be used during the Normandy operation. In addition, numerous support groups that were to prove vital to the success of the planned invasion of Europe began to arrive in the county. Among these personnel were air traffic controllers who would coordinate air support for the naval and land forces on D-Day. This work was to be done by Mobile Signal Units and it was decided that they should be trained at Chigwell.

In April the balloon centre at Chigwell was renamed RAF Chigwell and the number of personnel at the camp massively increased. Many of the newcomers had to sleep in bunk beds in unheated hangars with no plumbing.

While the raids continued in Essex some evacuees were still living in relative safety elsewhere in Britain. Terry Heather was now staying with his fourth family in Somerset and this was the strangest home yet for the boy from Dagenham. The man of the family made a living by making willow baskets. He had a large barn where the willow wands were left to dry. Terry was given the job of stripping the bark off the thin sticks before they could be used to make baskets. To supplement the family diet, the man would take his punt out at night and catch eels while Terry held a lamp. (The blackout was obviously not as rigorously applied in the countryside.) The family also shot birds of all kinds and ate them. Terry was often served a bird that he remembers as looking like a small chicken but he was never sure what it really was.

Every week a Blue Line coach turned up at Langport which the evacuees believed came from London. They would run alongside and watch as the passengers got off. One day Terry was surprised to see his mother. She was very unhappy with how her son was living and rented a local cottage where they both stayed for some time before returning to Dagenham.

March saw another transfer of war workers to Chelmsford. A number of young women were moved from the Midlands to work in the town's factories. Their arrival prompted an effort to find homes for the incomers, just as when the evacuees needed accommodation earlier in the war.

Often the noise of manufacturing was interrupted by a name called over the Tannoy system. The workforce would fall silent as someone went away to receive a telegram, often to read the news that a loved one had died on a battlefield far from Essex.

The *Essex County Standard* carried a Forces Column which reported on local men who were killed or missing – or in some cases enjoying themselves. Newspapers also

By 1943 many of the jobs at the Ford Motor Company in Dagenham were done by women. As well as producing military vehicles, the company also made engines for aircraft including Mosquitoes, Hurricanes and Lancasters. *(Ford Motor Company)*

regularly printed more detailed reports of local men who had died in action. Jack West, a cub master from Harold Wood, was reported missing after an RAF bombing raid. A Romford woman, Marjorie Morris, had not heard any news of her gunner husband, who was in Singapore, for fourteen months. She was then told that he was a prisoner of the Japanese. Major Charles Atfield Brooks of the Essex Regiment, who was from Dedham, had escaped from an Italian POW camp but was captured by the Germans after forty days of freedom.

Not all news of local servicemen was bad. An airman from Corbets Tey named Gamble Hayes received the Distinguished Flying Cross (DFC) from King George VI at Buckingham Palace for taking part in a daylight raid on Berlin which was responsible for delaying a speech by Göring. A Wrabness man told of a tank battle in Italy where the vehicles had to drive through water up to their turrets. This caused the loss of much of his crew's equipment which was stored outside the vehicle. It did not, however, stop them destroying a German tank. Mrs W. Mills of Colchester had a shock when she went to the cinema. During a newsreel she saw her son, Gunner Mills, in a film of the invasion of Sicily. He was holding a machine gun and smiling happily.

There was further proof that the population of some Essex towns was increasing because of the war. Donald Johnson stood as an independent candidate in an election in Chelmsford. He said he found the town crowded with people working very long hours in factories doing war work. Indeed, war workers were still continuing to pour into the county. In Dagenham there had been a shortage of voluntary billets for workers so compulsory billeting was introduced.

There was a general ban on building new homes as part of the drive to conserve labour and materials but allowances were made in some parts of the county. Under the Emergency War Programme, the construction of 3,000 cottages was planned for Lexden and Winstree. They were to be built in pairs at a cost of £850 per cottage. They had three bedrooms, electricity and a 120ft garden and were to be rented at 10s a week to farm workers.

Preparation for the invasion of Europe was going on in Tilbury at this time. A pipe was constructed that could be laid under the Channel to carry a constant supply of fuel for military vehicles from England to the Normandy coast. It was to be rolled off large drums installed on the back of ships.

In the months leading up to the Allied invasion, factories were constantly busy turning out the

Graves of members of the Essex Regiment grace many overseas cemeteries as well as those at home.

It seems that Americans were not the only soldiers with bars of chocolate. This is a wartime advertisement. *(Mars and Maltesers are registered trade marks. Used with permission from Mars UK Limited)*

" FIRST THINGS FIRST, FREDA "

MARS *comes first with the Forces*

materiel, transport and weapons the invasion force would need. The railway industry was also extremely busy, moving men around the country. By 1943 160,000 special trains had run since the outbreak of hostilities, carrying troops and their equipment.

In March there was a devastating event on the railway line from Fenchurch Street to Harwich. A train packed with servicemen and civilians fell into an enormous bomb crater after an explosive device landed on the line just as the locomotive approached. The accident happened between Shenfield and Ingatestone. Despite running at reduced speed, the engine tumbled into the hole killing the driver and fireman. Amazingly, only a few of the passengers were slightly injured. The railway staff were so efficient that by the following evening the line was open again.

In March, too, there was an example of the bravery of the pilots who had protected the country from the Luftwaffe, not that any further proof were really needed. An American pilot, Raimund Sanders Draper, was flying his Spitfire when the engine broke down. With no power he tried to land but was faced with the local junior and senior schools ahead of him. There seems to be no doubt that Draper gave his own life so as not to crash into the building. The institution was later renamed the Sanders Draper School.

A spectacularly visible dogfight took place in the sky over Clacton in April. It was the 20th, Hitler's birthday, when a Spitfire attacked a Junkers 88. At noon on the lovely clear day the battle was seen across much of Essex. In Colchester shoppers watched the fight and clapped and cheered as the German plane was shot down. During the course of the war a considerable number of German airmen were killed across the county. Thirty-six are buried in the cemetery in Becontree. Members of the RAF were often pallbearers at the burials.

Searchlights were fitted at Coalhouse Fort in April, along with Bofors anti-aircraft guns, which were part of the second line of defences, the first line being nearer the coast. As well as defence against air raids, the fort also had water-borne protection in the form of an electronic minefield in the River Thames. Barbed wire was used as land defences outside Coalhouse Fort, along with trenches and pillboxes on the riverbank. Further inland there were several positions to command roads in case an invading force should get past the fort. The regular army presence at Coalhouse was reinforced by 356 Coast Battery Home Guard Detachment.

There seems to have been a change in the attitude of some Home Guard members by this stage of the war. Numerous reports appeared in the newspapers about how Home Guard members were being charged with not reporting for duty. In Romford three privates were fined for this offence. At Warley Barracks a member of the 5th Battalion Essex Home Guard was court-martialled for using insub-

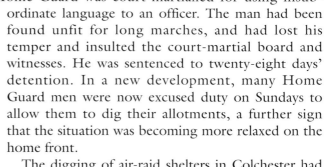

ordinate language to an officer. The man had been found unfit for long marches, and had lost his temper and insulted the court-martial board and witnesses. He was sentenced to twenty-eight days' detention. In a new development, many Home Guard men were now excused duty on Sundays to allow them to dig their allotments, a further sign that the situation was becoming more relaxed on the home front.

The digging of air-raid shelters in Colchester had led to the discovery of numerous previously un-known Roman remains. Archaeological finds were also made in the aftermath of air raids. A bomb that landed by the castle revealed traces of a Roman road.

The tower at Walton-on-the-Naze. Although it dated back hundreds of years, this building came into use as a lookout post and later as a radar tower during the Second World War. There had been calls for it to be demolished because it was such a clear landmark for enemy planes.

Just like everyone else, the Dagenham Girl Pipers had to be prepared for enemy attacks. It must have been very difficult, however, to play bagpipes in a gas mask. *(Dagenham Girl Pipers)*

Although air-raid shelters were an important part of life at this time, that did not stop some youngsters from vandalising them. The problem got so bad in Hornchurch, where nineteen shelters were damaged, that there were calls to allow entry into shelters only during the raids. Councillor Mrs Sherring said that shelters should be treated with the same level of respect as a church.

It was not only male hooligans who were causing problems: there were calls for approved schools for female delinquents. Some people were against this idea because it might place vulnerable girls under the influence of hardened offenders. Building such institutions would give the courts somewhere to put these girls but it did not solve the problem of how to give them good parents, the critics said. They argued for the use of fostering instead.

By this stage of the war most factory workers were women, and women were taking a more active role in areas of public life too. Romford now had four female councillors and in Colchester women were involved in the defence of the town through the formation of a female Home Guard unit. Officially they had no connection with the real Home Guard, but they numbered over 150 in strength and had four rifles. Some members belonged to Colchester Rifle Club and took part in shooting competitions.

There is no doubt that the war had a huge effect on women. They were forced to leave home and take a bigger part in society. One result was that they gained more confidence. Young girls who went to live in hostels with others learned more about life than they ever did at home with their parents. Things that seem normal now were major events in wartime, such as the fact that women could wear trousers without inviting comment. Of course not all the developments that resulted from this emancipation were positive. Illegitimate births multiplied, as did the number of sexually transmitted diseases. However, this trend did bring about greater openness in dealing with such matters. The government was forced to open public discussions on the treatment of STDs. Pregnancy among unmarried women also became less of a stigma than it had been in pre-war years.

Even after four years the blackout was still a hazard for the residents of Essex. One woman lost her bearings in the darkness and fell in the River Colne in Colchester. Luckily a passing soldier heard her cries for help, managed to find her and got her back on to dry land.

Still looking for new employees to keep up with the demands of war work, one company had the idea of reinforcing its workforce by employing fifty Italian prisoners of war. They lived in a YMCA building outside the main gate of May & Baker's chemical works in Dagenham. (May & Baker was not the only place where Italian POWs were put to work. Many of the farms in the Thurrock area used Italians as labourers. They lived at Camp 286 in Purfleet.)

Although most recreational facilities had been abandoned at May & Baker during the conflict, netball, badminton and tennis were still played. The company also continued to hold a sports day. Moreover, the drama club remained in full swing and asked for new premises. In an unheard of move, the Ministry of Supply finally agreed to allow the building of a new canteen inside the factory, complete with a stage. Soon after completion a V1 landed close to the new building and smashed all its windows.

Entertainment was an important part of maintaining morale during the war and companies involved in the industry continued to do their best to make money and to expand. Odeon took over numerous cinemas in Essex in the war years. In 1943 alone it acquired the Havana and the Plaza in Romford, the Tower in Hornchurch, the Capital in Upminster, the Grange in Dagenham, the Regent in Becontree, the Rio in Barking and the Savoy in Ilford. By this point the company owned over 300 cinemas.

For the first years of the war rationing had worked well but in May 1943 the system was as close as it ever came to failure. New ration books and identity cards were to be issued, and the rules said that the new cards had to be collected from the Food Office in Colchester. The 23,000 books had to be distributed at the rate of 1,000 a day to achieve the target of completion by 25 July, but in fact only 300 were given out. Local officials ignored the rules, sorted books into batches for each village and then went out to deliver them instead.

At one stage some fishmongers called for fish to be rationed. It was reported that many shoppers travelled great distances to buy fish when it was not available in the area in which they lived. In Romford shoppers came from as far afield as Chelmsford, and there were calls for fishmongers to be allowed to ask for proof that customers were local before selling to them.

The Civic Restaurants were another source of unrationed food. In Hornchurch the local council decided that meals could be provided for some retired people for 6*d*. This service was available to those who were on pensions of less than £1 a week.

Incidents still occurred in Essex's biggest centres of population that seem to be more in keeping with a rural backwater than a thriving urban area. At Chelmsford a cow escaped from the market and, unlike the comical results of Colchester's rampaging bull a few years earlier, this incident had serious consequences. The cow ended up in the garden of a house in Springfield Road where it knocked over the daughter of the house owner. The girl hit her head on a step and died.

In May the government decided that local councils should begin to plan for meeting a postwar housing shortage. A scheme was drawn up in Chelmsford to construct a number of dwellings to meet the expected shortfall.

In July a campaign was launched against the Essex War Agricultural Committee. This organisation had the power to take over land from farmers. The opposition group, the Essex Farmers' and Country People's Association, called for an inquiry by the Ministry of Agriculture into the workings of the committee. Its demands included the introduction of an appeals system, a new rule that only one member of a family could sit on the committee's board and the restriction that no confiscated land could be given to a friend or relative of a committee member or to members themselves. It seems that public feelings were running high and there was considerable suspicion of those in power.

Crime was still rife in the county and even air raids were seen as an opportunity by some less than honest members of the public. One man was sentenced to fifteen months at Chelmsford for stealing goods. He was suspected of looting from shops that were damaged in a raid.

Laws introduced because of the war continued to lead to prosecutions. A Romford man was fined £5 for feeding bread that was fit for human consumption to his chickens. A Collier Row woman was charged with failing to alert the authorities of the arrival of an alien in the area – she had an Austrian friend to stay for the weekend. She pleaded ignorance of the law.

A Hornchurch man refused to attend an army medical and was charged with avoiding military service. He argued that he was not a con-scientious objector and had in fact been in the army before. After leaving the forces he had been unable to find work. Then he could not find anywhere for his wife to live. He argued that the way he had been treated led him to think that the country was not worth fighting for.

The arrival of the Americans made a big impression on the female population of the

THE MATCH FOR THE
BRITISH FORCES
BRITISH MADE BY BRYANT & MAY

Bryant & May gave up its sports ground for the war effort but the business carried on. This is a wartime advertisement.

county. The US was the place where films shown in the cinema came from and American servicemen were seen as part of this romantic, glamorous scene. It was not only older girls who came under American influence. Chelmsford juvenile court took two girls of thirteen and fourteen into care because they were associating with US servicemen and were considered to be in moral danger. This was not an isolated case. There are examples of Americans being charged with offences against young girls. Some were reportedly jailed as a result.

It would seem that it was not only young girls who had something to fear from some American personnel. A taxi driver left home telling his landlady that he had a job for two American soldiers. He was not seen again until his body was found in a ditch on the Maldon road. Two black American servicemen were later questioned about the murder.

In 1943 the Bishop of Chelmsford had much to say about what was happening in wartime Britain. It was not only moral standards that concerned him. He said in a column in an Essex newspaper that higher living standards, better pensions, insurance and social services seemed to have improved life for most people. However, he questioned whether the population was any happier than it had been in Victorian times. This seems a strange point to make given that most of those who lived through the war saw it as a happy time.

The pursuit of organised sport was almost non-existent during the war years. The football leagues were suspended and Colchester United were disbanded. In the 1943/4 season, however, the army team began to play at Layer Road as the Colchester Garrison XI. They included England internationals such as Ralph Birkett, normally of Newcastle but based in Colchester, and also Scottish internationals including Dave McCulloch, normally of Derby County. The army side became almost as popular as Colchester United had been.

Like footballers, top-class cricket players were also based in Colchester and the garrison team's members included D. Smith of Derbyshire and England, F. Hawker of Essex and Gloucestershire's Lambert.

There were more attempts at promoting leisure activities in Colchester. The Wardens' Social Club organised a funfair in Castle Park as part of the town's Holiday at Home scheme. There were also band concerts, singing sessions, PT displays and firefighting demonstrations, all to entertain a public starved of fun.

Many young people managed to get a holiday of sorts when over 2,000 army cadets attended training at Colchester Camp. These camps lasted for three weeks in July and August.

Towards the end of the year the first British prisoners of war came home. These were wounded men who had travelled by ship from Germany and landed at Liverpool. Essex servicemen were among them.

Local men serving in the Middle East received a message from home in late 1943. A radio van toured Romford interviewing people, including stallholders in the market and the organist at St Edward's church. The interviews and news of the area were made into a half-hour programme which was broadcast to British forces in the Middle East.

SEVEN

1944: Germany is Bombed and D-Day Arrives

By January 1944 roles were reversed from the position during the Battle of Britain: now German cities were receiving continual bombardment. In February final plans were made for D-Day, which was scheduled for late May or early June. There were problems, however, involving General de Gaulle and the Free French, who did not agree on the timing of the proposed landings.

The war in Italy was not going well: the Anzio landing force had become bogged down and a fierce, drawn-out series of battles at Monte Cassino lasted from January to May.

March saw an unusual event on the home front, given the attempts made by almost the whole population to help the war effort since the outbreak of hostilities: there was industrial unrest when miners went on unofficial strike to demand higher wages. It began in Wales and spread to Scotland. Not until the end of the month were the miners persuaded to return to work.

German settlers who had moved into Poland after the invasion began to flee back to Germany in fear of the advancing Russians.

In April half a million extra American troops arrived in Britain in preparation for D-Day. They quickly discovered the dangers of the blackout and realised how easy it was to be involved in road accidents. There were also problems with the treatment of black American servicemen. Segregation was the norm in the USA but it was strongly resisted in Britain.

The turning point in the battle for Italy came in May. The Germans finally began to retreat, allowing the Allies to move on Rome. Then on 6 June – D-Day – Allied forces began to land in Normandy and it was the beginning of the end for the Germans.

Invasion did not, however, signal peace for the civilian population. In June, Hitler unleashed his secret weapon, the doodlebug or V1. This weapon was followed by the even more deadly V2, which brought a fresh terror to a population who thought that they had braved the worst the Germans could throw at them. However, one small positive story did emerge from the introduction of the new weapon: when a rocket landed on Howard's chemical works in Ilford the remains were used to produce sulphate of iron.

The Ministry of Agriculture sent out a new message to encourage the population to continue with the Dig for Victory campaign. The end of the war might have been in sight but complacency was to be avoided; food would still be in short supply after hostilities ceased.

There were two big events in September 1944: Paris was finally liberated and by the end of the month the invasion of Holland had begun. October saw a meeting between Winston Churchill, the Foreign Secretary Anthony Eden and Stalin. It was at this meeting that the future of eastern Europe was agreed by dividing the area into spheres of influence. However, Roosevelt was not happy when he heard what had been agreed. The Allies continued to make progress in mainland Europe and Athens was liberated in October.

By November the remaining U-boats had been destroyed. Most were lost trying to stop the Allied invasion. Many of their bases had also been captured. Elsewhere, the Russian Army had taken Romania, Bulgaria and Yugoslavia and was now attacking Hungary.

December saw the standing down of the Home Guard. The threat of invasion was over and there was no longer any need for the organisation. Over 7,000 members marched through London and were told by their Colonel-in-Chief, King George VI, that they had fulfilled their task.

In mainland Europe the Allies were finally inside Germany, but by Christmas there was civil war in Greece.

After escaping relatively lightly throughout the war, Colchester was hit very hard in February 1944 when incendiary bombs fell, starting fires that destroyed numerous houses, factories and shops around St Boltoph's station.

Criminals who escape sentencing on legal technicalities might seem to be a modern phenomenon, but this also happened during the war. A woman was murdered in Southend and the man found guilty of the crime was sentenced to death. He already had a conviction for manslaughter, and yet his conviction was later overturned on account of the way the trial had been conducted.

A war-related crime was committed in Rainham. Two sixteen-year-old boys stole a Sten gun, two rifles and hundreds of rounds of ammunition from a Home Guard hut in the cemetery in Upminster Road. In Colchester a woman was sent to prison for three months for stealing £2 from an American soldier. He had wanted to buy a bottle of gin and the woman said she could get one for £2. He gave her the money and she disappeared.

In March the Germans planned an air attack on the Marconi factory in Chelmsford. This was a reprisal for the RAF raid on Philips' Eindhoven factory. Fighters from Bradwell shot down the first five Junkers bombers, which were the pathfinders, and saved the factory. When the Allies later invaded Germany they found a model of the Marconi works at a German airbase. It had been used to plan the raid.

During March many road signs were returned to major routes through the country. The German threat had relaxed but April nevertheless saw an increase in the scope of the restricted area along the Essex coast as preparations for D-Day got under way. Two of the areas that now came under the regulations were Hornchurch and Brentwood. The Essex Regiment was moved out of its base at Warley Barracks for the first time in over sixty years and sent to a commandeered holiday camp in Blackpool. Warley was to be used as a troop assembly area for D-Day.

Inhabitants of restricted areas were not drastically affected by the regulations. The families of residents were allowed to visit but a fine of up to £100 could be imposed on anyone found in controlled areas without good cause. There were no roadblocks but regular police patrols were made at strategic points.

The increase in the size of the restricted areas caused panic among many residents. They were worried that the large troop movements would disrupt the normal transport of food. There was also the added burden of trying to feed the thousands of servicemen pouring into the county. Considering the huge numbers of people involved, it is surprising that in the event there was little disruption to civilian food supplies.

From late May the Thames became an assembly area for vessels being made ready for the Normandy landings, including the Mulberry harbours, which were to be assembled on the French beaches. There was a police crackdown in the controlled area along the Thames and thirteen people were arrested and fined £1 for not carrying their identity cards.

The Thames had now been invaded by the Americans and ships flying the Stars and Stripes were as common as British vessels. The tank landing ships were among the strangest sights. These craft had been designed in England but built in America. They held thirty tanks and had a front that opened up like a set of giant's jaws to allow the vehicles to drive ashore.

So many ships crowded the river that there was insufficient room for them all at the docks and jetties. There were lines of craft of all sizes moored in the middle of the Thames, waiting their turn to pull into the shore and load up with men and machines. The number of new ships grew with each month: between January and March 3,256 arrived, from April to June 4,950 and between July and September 5,186. Sitting among the larger vessels were smaller boats, such as the ferries from Harwich. Some of these had been involved in the Dunkirk evacuation and once again many men from Harwich were to die doing their duty.

Essex itself was full of men waiting to board the ships. The camps and barracks of the county were full to overflowing. The A13 road was closed to the public and was lined with military vehicles being made ready for the invasion. Every spare piece of land was full of soldiers. Tented camps were set up at Belhus Park, South Ockendon, and at Orsett on what is now the golf course. There was even a camp inside Tilbury Docks.

Terry Heather found the war very much in evidence when he returned to Dagenham from evacuation in Somerset. The family had an Anderson shelter in the garden, in which he often slept. The doorway was covered in sacking and he

John Smith with members of his regiment and local children in Bombay. John is second from right. *(John Smith)*

remembers the structure had a strong musty smell. He also spent many nights sleeping in the cupboard under the stairs. He recalls the terrible feeling of being woken up in the middle of the night and rushed down into the shelter.

As the war was a much greater part of his life now, Terry became involved in action with his friends. The youngsters in his area formed their own junior Home Guard and had an old bayonet which they practised stabbing into telegraph poles. They also had a disarmed grenade to throw. The war was much closer to home than when he had been evacuated. There were now anti-aircraft guns in Parsloes Park. Terry also remembers seeing a doodlebug pass overhead and land on the public toilets in Lodge Avenue. He rushed to the scene and found a huge crater with damaged houses on each side of it. One house had lost its front wall. The memory has stayed with him because the property looked like a doll's house, the front open so he could see into all the rooms.

Sylvia Walker also had experience of a doodlebug in Dagenham. The family ran down into their shelter as the rocket came over. Sylvia's mother threw the children into the shelter and lay on top of them. Sylvia recollects hearing the droning of the engine of the bomb which, once it stopped, would fall from the sky and cause disaster. She remembers a V1 falling on Martin's Corner and a V2 on Parsloes Park.

On one occasion Sylvia's father came home on leave from the army. During a raid he went into the house to make the family some cocoa. Because of the blackout he could not see what he was doing and put Bisto into the cups instead of cocoa.

Strange coincidences were reported involving local men on active service. Two brothers from Romford, Joseph and Albert Duke, who had not seen each other for some time met while they were both serving in Italy. Another set of brothers from Harold Wood also met up far from the county, but not in happy circumstances. William Terry, a rifleman with the London Irish Rifles, had been serving in Sicily. His brother Clifford was in the Royal Artillery and they were reunited in a prisoner-of-war camp in Austria. It was not only brothers from the Romford area that met abroad. Sidney and Douglas Scott from Colchester were reunited in the Middle East.

Other local servicemen were engaged at sea. H. Standing of Collier Row and Tom Lever of Gidea Park were serving on HMS *Enterprise*, which, along with HMS *Glasgow*, sank three German destroyers in the Bay of Biscay. The *Romford Times* also carried a photograph of sixteen local men in the crew of a 'certain cruiser', which was serving with Admiral James Somerville's fleet. Meanwhile, Captain D. Wilkie of Hornchurch, a medical officer, was mentioned in dispatches for gallantry when he was wounded while being dive-bombed close to Tripoli. W. Williamson, a footballer for Romford, was killed on active service.

The families of servicemen were not all waiting patiently at home for their menfolk. The wife of an RAF man, who was living in Hornchurch, was sentenced to fourteen days in prison for abandoning her children aged seven and five.

When the people of Southend and the surrounding districts woke on the morning of 6 June they found that most of the ships previously moored in the Thames Estuary had disappeared. They had sailed in the night, six different convoys heading for France.

Many Essex inhabitants had already guessed that the invasion was about to get under way, but if proof were needed, on the night of 6 June the air over Essex was filled with hoards of planes, some towing gliders.

The following day an invasion communiqué was posted in the window of the *Essex County Standard* office. Days later the newspaper carried front-page headlines about the low-flying aircraft skimming the Essex rooftops. It also reported how all main roads in the Colchester area were filled with the roar of passing convoys.

However, the secrecy of D-Day had been maintained in the weeks leading up to 6 June. Anyone crossing the barriers set up at American airbases was detained until the invasion was under way. Many civilians from Colchester working at an American site were kept in the camp until a special air mission had been completed. The Americans were very apologetic but those detained reported they had been treated kindly and were so well fed that they did not want to be released.

Radio broadcasts announcing the invasion were received with a mixture of emotions. There was joy at the news of a step towards the defeat of the Germans, but there was anxiety too. Churches in the county stayed open all day on 6 June so that local people could pray for their men who were involved in the landings.

COUNTY BOROUGH OF SOUTHEND-ON-SEA.
AIR RAID PRECAUTIONS DEPARTMENT.

120, Victoria Avenue,
SOUTHEND-ON-SEA.

D/L.
Circ.No.705.   7th March, 1944.

Read and
Signed.   Children's Respirators.

As you are aware children's respirators, subject to
the fittings suitable for individual children, are normally
required for children between the ages of 18/20 months
and 4/4½ years.

The Minister of Home Security points out that the
number of children's respirators which have been issued to
this Authority substantially exceed the numbers in the age
group 1½ to 4½ years.   It can, therefore, only be concluded
that these respirators are being retained unnecessarily for
children after they reach the age of, say 4½ years, or that
children's respirators are not being recovered when adult
respirators are issued.

The drain on the Supply Department's stocks of these
respirators is becoming serious and the time is not far
distant when the Minister will be compelled to stop further
supplies for a time.   He does not, however, desire that
the position should deteriorate to that extent and he looks
to the members of the Wardens' Service to ensure the recovery
of all children's respirators which are replaced by adult
respirators and to hasten the exchange of children's
respirators for small adult respirators as soon as the
growth of the child warrants it.

Air Raid Precautions Officer.

TO:

Senior Staff Officers.
Staff Officers to the Chief Warden.
Assistant Staff Officers to the Chief Warden.
Head Wardens.
Deputy Head Wardens.
Senior Wardens.

The authorities were obviously worried about the number of gas masks that had been handed
out in the Southend area. There was a shortage in 1944.

A painting by a member of the St Osyth's History Society showing how the sky above Essex was full of planes during the invasion of Europe. *(St Osyth's Local History Society)*

Three days later the ships began to return from Normandy. This time the men they carried were German prisoners. Many were landed at Tilbury and sent to Camps 654 and 655 in nearby Purfleet. Some of the Essex camps for Germans were built by Italian POWs who were already here.

The arrival of so many prisoners of war was not without problems. In Colchester three Germans escaped from a camp. They were all wearing jackboots, which must have looked very suspicious. They were captured after four days. A man was also fined £5 at Colchester for selling a POW twenty cigarettes.

Italian prisoners of war had been allowed quite high levels of freedom in many parts of the county, so much so that they were permitted to attend dances at Saffron Walden town hall. That is until American servicemen complained about their presence. There were also complaints from British servicemen stationed overseas. They argued that it was not right that Italians were allowed to mix socially with British women when a short time ago they had been killing British men. The mayor of the town banned POWs from any further dances.

Many of the vessels used to transport those who had been wounded on the beaches of Normandy and prisoners of war to Essex after D-Day did not stay long. They loaded up with more men and equipment and returned to France. The number of ships that left the River Thames was greater after D-Day than on 6 June.

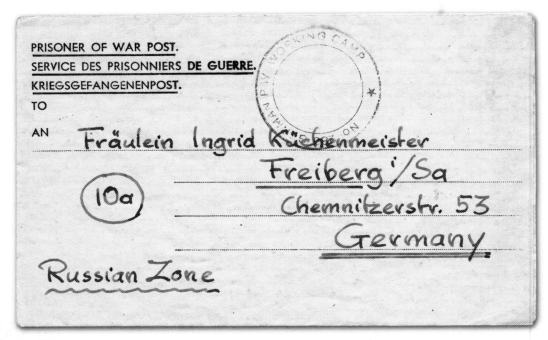

PRISONER OF WAR POST.
SERVICE DES PRISONNIERS DE GUERRE.
KRIEGSGEFANGENENPOST.

TO

AN   *Fräulein Ingrid Küchenmeister*

Freiberg i/Sa

(10a)   *Chemnitzerstr. 53*

Germany.

Russian Zone

The Essex countryside became the site of numerous POW camps after D-Day as German prisoners were brought back across the Channel. This is a letter from a German prisoner at Camp 286 in Purfleet.

Vessels also began to bring back the wounded from the beaches of Normandy. Newspapers carried the stories of a number of Essex men. The *Romford Times* printed a front-page photograph of Lance-Corporal Edward Balles of Dagenham being treated for his wounds in Oldchurch Hospital, Romford.

Regular reports of bombing raids continued to appear in the press. Exact locations were never named, but the *Romford Times* reported that schools, a cinema and a hospital were damaged in 'a south-east town'; a 55-year-old warden, F.W. Garwood, was killed in the raid. The report of bomb damage to 'a brewery' must have made many readers suspect that Romford Brewery had been hit, and not for the first time.

The Allied forces landed in Normandy in June and doodlebugs began to fall in England the same month. Joan Francis was married by this time and had moved to digs in South Woodford because her husband was stationed close by. She experienced her first doodlebug in South Woodford, an engine sound that was quite different from any aircraft she had ever heard. The next day rumours were rife that it had been a pilotless plane, but doodlebugs soon became a part of everyday life. Joan describes them as 'a hateful psychological weapon'. When the engine cut the waiting seemed endless for those below. Some V1s glided away, some fell straight down. Joan says they were the first things that really scared her during the war.

One night a doodlebug fell near Joan's digs while she was sleeping under a large dining table. The impact left her deaf for three days. A cot previously used by a baby in the house was covered with broken glass and the landlord who slept on the hearthrug was covered in soot. When Joan arrived at work the next day all the windows were smashed.

Soon after, Joan was transferred to a farm in Beaumont and lived with friends because she was now nearer her home in Thorpe-le-Soken. As the only Land Girl there she had to do muck-spreading using a pitchfork, which she found very boring. Threshing was also tedious; catching chaff in a sack left her covered in dust. When it rained she was a skivvy to the farmer's wife.

The German deployment of doodlebugs had a great effect on Romford. In July, the month after the weapons started to fall, women and children were evacuated from the town for the first time in the war. Nearly 10,000 people left the area, mainly for Suffolk and Norfolk. New rounds of evacuation occurred in many parts of Essex, especially the areas closer to London.

Romford Brewery suffered bomb damage on a number of occasions. This raid took place in 1940.

The village of Copford was denied an air-raid siren and so became the first place in the country to provide its own. Not that it was much use against doodlebug attacks. The *Essex County Standard* described how the engines on the flying bombs cut out miles from where they landed, so quiet country lanes knew nothing of what was approaching until the explosion. One report told of how a three-year-old girl slept in bed as her house was wrecked by a doodlebug. The first she knew about it was when her mother woke her. There was also a story about how the first casualties caused by a flying bomb occurred in one 'area of southern England'. Four people were killed in a village when four thatched cottages were destroyed.

Because of the new threat from flying bombs large numbers of anti-aircraft gunners and searchlight troops were moved to remote east coast sites. Here they often had to live in tents until huts were built for them. Their job was to shoot down the bombs as they crossed the coastline.

Jimmy Underwood finally got home to find out what was happening in Essex when he was given leave from HMS *Nigeria* in 1944. He found the situation just as dangerous at home as it was on his ship. While he was with a friend in Elephant and Castle he saw his first doodlebug and thought that it was an aircraft on fire because of the smoke coming out of it. Then it landed and blew him through a shop window. He was left with a large piece of glass sticking out of his hand. Jimmy had another unpleasant experience back home in Dagenham while he was on leave. He was just going out of the Church Elm pub in the Heathway when a bomb landed on the Fifty Shillings Tailors opposite and blew him back through the doors of the pub. The shop was next to the site of the greengrocer's stall where Jimmy used to work. He remembers that after the bomb landed, many of the suits and jackets from the tailor's shop quickly disappeared as locals ran off with them. After his experiences on leave he was happy to get back to his ship.

In Colchester there were attempts to bring visiting troops and those from Britain together. An Allies Club was opened by the WVS. In addition to the 400 soldiers enrolled as members, 100 young women were allowed to join. It seems that it was another opportunity for the Americans to meet Essex girls.

Strangely, at the same time that people were being evacuated from towns like Romford, visits to some seaside areas were being permitted once more. This seems to show that flying-bomb attacks were concentrated on the area around the capital rather than near the coast.

In other parts of the county concerts, competitions and outdoor events were organised in support of Save the Soldier Week. Several campaigns of this nature were run during the war, including War Weapons Week and Warship Week.

The newspapers continued to carry reports of how families were doing all they could for the war effort, which were no doubt attempts to raise morale in the face of the new bombing threat. The Jones family from Chadwell Heath were reported to be very proud of their three sons who serving in the army. Another son worked in munitions. They also had a daughter in the ATS and two more in war factories. Mr Jones had done his bit by serving in the First World War.

By September thirty-six V1s had fallen on Barking. Many landed harmlessly in the marshes but others hit populated areas and several people died. A rocket landed in St Ann's Road damaging 1,500 houses but, incredibly, it did not kill anyone. Over 60 per cent of the total housing stock in the town was damaged by enemy bombing.

In September the invasion of Holland began and signs of the event were clear in the county. The fleet of gliders on its way to Holland was so large that it took more than an hour and a half to fly over Brightlingsea.

As 1944 wore on there were further relaxations in the limits put on travel to restricted areas. In September the ban on outsiders entering Colchester was lifted. This led to a rush of people arriving to visit friends and family.

In October another doodlebug arrived in Romford marketplace but this time it was on the back of a lorry. It was exhibited by the National Fire Service during a drive to raise funds. Thousands of people came to look at the object of terror and donated over £100.

November saw the beginning of the end of many home front obligations. The 8th Battalion Essex Home Guard held a farewell parade of over 1,000 members. Lieutenant-General Sir Geoffrey Howard, the Colonel of the Essex Regiment, thanked the men for their service.

There was an attempt to entertain troops who were based in Colchester but no longer taking an active part in the war. The wounded and returning prisoners of war were given half-price seats and free teas at the Regal Cinema on Tuesday afternoons. In what might today seem a strange move, hospital patients were given free cigarettes.

Any plans to relax the duties of the ARP wardens were forgotten because of the V2 rockets, which began to arrive in a final wave of spite from the almost-defeated Germans. November did, however, see a relaxation of the blackout in some parts of Essex.

The same month the newspapers carried a tragic story that was not related to the war. A three-year-old boy from Colchester fell into a hole that was full of water. The treatment he received at the Essex County Hospital seems primitive now – he was placed in an iron lung. Unfortunately, it did no good and the child died.

The proximity of Christmas did little to deter enemy action. On 19 December the Hoffman ball-bearing factory at Chelmsford took a direct hit from a V2. Forty people died, including twenty-nine workers who had just been singing Christmas carols with members of the Salvation Army. American servicemen were among the first to arrive to aid the injured.

Although the end of the war may have been in sight, Terry Heather's family decided that he should be sent away from Dagenham again because of the danger from both V1s and then V2s. This time, however, he went to his aunt's house in Wisbech. Once again Terry had to get used to a different way of life. He remembers that country people did not use the front door or the parlour. They would live almost entirely in the kitchen, sitting on hard wooden chairs. There was no mains electricity or running water in the area. Lighting was by oil lamp and water came from a large cistern outside the back door. The radio was powered by a large battery with handles. Every family had two of these batteries, and as one ran down it would be taken to the local garage where the other had been on charge and swapped over.

Wisbech people seemed never to leave their local surroundings. They grew their own food and kept chickens for eggs. The milkman came in a pony and trap and sold milk from a large churn using a ladle. The war seemed far away because many of the local men were excused service because they worked on the land.

It was not unusual for men to work all day on farms and then go out again after dinner for a few more hours' pea or potato picking. Terry managed to find different employment: he pumped the organ in church on Sundays and was paid 10*s* a quarter. By the time the war ended Terry was due to leave school. He posed a problem in the locality: all young men went into farming while all girls went into service and Terry wanted to be an engineer.

He found work at Dobson's agricultural engineers as a stores boy. He was so scared of the boss that he agreed to start on the Monday despite not leaving school officially until Wednesday. On Tuesday the school board man came round and he had to go back to school for the last two days. He travelled the 7 miles to Dobson's on his aunt's bicycle, a woman's bike with a basket on the front. He had an army haversack in which he carried his sandwiches and a bottle of cold cocoa.

Although those serving in the forces had received a 'statutory assurance' that their jobs would be open to them when they returned, this was only applicable to the able-bodied. There was a huge problem of how to help those who had returned from the war disabled. During the earlier years of the conflict many people with disabilities had been found employment: they were an untapped supply of labour that had been ignored during times of high unemployment before 1939. The introduction of disabled people into the workplace and the increase in the number of those permanently physically affected by the war led to the Disabled Persons Act, which did much to carry on the good work that had begun during hostilities.

Christmas 1944 was marked by a great shortage of anything worth buying. This resulted in enormously high prices for any item, even second-hand toys. Doll's prams sold for nearly £20 and train sets were not much cheaper. Turkeys were supposedly sold at a controlled price of 3*s* 2*d* a pound. However, there was a severe shortage of the poultry and black market birds fetched nearer 10*s* a pound.

Some children did very well that Christmas because Canadian servicemen had saved up their sweet ration to give to them. The Americans were famous for the lavish parties they laid on for children as well. At an Eighth Air Force fighter base personnel had been donating sweets for weeks before Christmas and this meant that over 200 local children could be treated to a party. The men had also been sent toys and games from home which were given to the children. A Walt Disney cartoon was shown at the camp cinema, but no doubt the ride to the base in American trucks had been just as exciting for the children. There were reports of many other US bases doing the same. In return, local people once again invited servicemen into their homes for Christmas.

EIGHT

1945: The End is Near . . . for Some

January 1945 saw the fall of Warsaw to the Russians and by the end of the month Russian forces were entering Germany. They treated the German population brutally in revenge for what had happened in Russia.

In February Churchill, Stalin and Roosevelt met at Yalta in the Crimea to discuss various war issues, in particular how postwar Germany would be governed. At home the Barrage Balloon Command, now run almost entirely by WAAFs, was disbanded.

In March the German Army's desperation became clear as it began to send fifteen- and sixteen-year-old boys to the front line. German soldiers were now so short of weapons that they tried to buy black market arms in Italy. This month also saw the last German bombing raid on Britain – RAF bases were attacked.

Belsen was liberated in April. Allied forces made the local population visit the camp to witness what had been going on there. Many Allied prisoners of war were also freed at this time, including those in Colditz Castle. April also saw the sudden death of President Roosevelt. He was replaced by President Truman.

While the Russians were still fighting in Berlin, German radio announced that Adolf Hitler had committed suicide, along with Eva Braun and Joseph Goebbels. The city surrendered on 2 May, the German High Command following suit on the 7th.

In July the Labour Party under Clement Attlee won a landslide victory in Britain's General Election. There was also a meeting of Allied leaders in Berlin to discuss the use of the atomic bomb against Japan. The first H-bomb was dropped on Hiroshima on 6 August. The second fell on Nagasaki on the 9th. Finally, on 15 August, Victory in Japan Day was announced.

On 20 November the first sitting of the International Military Tribunal to try war crimes took place in Nuremberg. As a result of its judgments many of the men involved in running the concentration camps were hanged.

The year 1945 started with the coldest spell since 1940. This was made worse in Colchester by the fact that gas and electricity supplies were turned off because of shortages.

Also in Colchester, the Goodridge family were homeless and had been since D-Day. Their home and everything in it had been destroyed when a Bren-gun carrier full of explosives blew up as it drove past. The family complained that the explosion was 'the wrong nationality' – if it had been caused by enemy action they would have been compensated, but because it was the result of an accident involving British weapons, they were still fighting for compensation.

Although there were a few final V-bomb attacks on the county early in the year, there were no serious raids in 1945. The *Romford Times* announced that it was time to put aside the 'Security Curtain' and show how local areas had stood up to the final onslaught by the defeated German Army.

The V1 attacks had lasted 80 days and the V2 bombings 200 days; some 57 deaths occurred as a result of the 100 bombs that fell on the locality. Winston Churchill mentioned Essex in one of his speeches. He described it as one of the most bombed counties of Britain. The *Essex County Standard* was now able to report that one of the first rockets had fallen on Weeley in November 1944.

War-related deaths were not entirely restricted to air attacks at this late stage of the conflict. A mine killed two boys on the beach at Mersea Island. The boys, aged sixteen and seventeen, were out shooting rabbits when they strayed into a mined area. In another incident, George Smith, aged fourteen, told how his friend Peter Bleakly of Layer-de-la-Haye died when he picked up a hand grenade which then exploded. The boys found the grenade on a farm. Frank Taylor, a wounded soldier from Romford, was at a lecture on mines at an army camp in Kent. The lecturer used a live mine for demonstration purposes; it exploded and killed twenty men. Another soldier, Arthur Harrington from Upminster, drowned in an army camp in Feltham, Middlesex.

The advance of the Allies towards Berlin was welcome news for the population of Essex, but many of those at home were still concerned for loved ones caught up in the final stages of the war. Although many prisoners of war had returned to the UK from camps already liberated, others had not. The families of POWs imprisoned in Germany were worried by the lack of news coming out of the country. When liberated men attended a meeting of the Friends of POWs Guild in Dagenham in March, there must have been mixed feelings among them. Many of their comrades were still in Germany or were prisoners of the Japanese. There had always been great local support for POWs. The Red Cross store in Romford marketplace had been open since April 1943. Goods in the shop could be purchased by relatives and then parcelled up and sent to the camps.

Although the war was as good as over, there was a final call for the people of Colchester to offer their spare rooms to strangers. In previous years they had been asked to take in evacuees, old people and war workers. Now they were asked to give lodgings to prisoners of war from the Empire who had been brought back to England before being sent back to their own countries.

The final chapters of the war in Europe were well reported in the newspapers, but peacetime events began to outweigh the horrors of the conflict. Sailing was finally allowed again on the Thames Estuary. Civil defence stations were stood down – for example, the Bull Lane Civil Defence Depot in Dagenham closed and its duties were taken over by other Dagenham depots. Farewell parties were held at fire guard posts as the men reported for duty for the final time.

The war still had a sting in its tail, however. On the same page as its story about the closure of fire stations, the *Romford Times* reported that six people had died in a V-bomb attack.

Secrecy still surrounded some news coverage. Despite reporting a serious fire at the Sterling Refrigerator Company in Dagenham, which was fought by workers, the newspapers never mentioned that the factory was producing machine guns at the time.

Some people were still being punished for war-related crimes in the spring of 1945. A deserter was arrested in Colchester carrying a forged ID card. The woman he lived with was charged with supplying him with the card and they were both sentenced to three months in prison.

That the end of the war was on the horizon was evident when twenty-seven Essex children arrived home from Canada. They had been evacuated there after the fall of France and had stayed with Ford employees. Some were only five years old when they left and now returned with much of their childhood gone.

Over 300 children who had stayed in the UK were treated to a party attended by the mayor at Wykham Hall, Romford. They were all either bomb victims or the children of those in the services. Meanwhile, the Public Assistance Committee in Chelmsford launched a scheme to find 'uncles' and 'aunts' to befriend orphans who had lost their parents in the war. These friends would take the youngsters on outings and bring them gifts as a way of making their lives in children's homes more normal.

Bill Dudley was only a toddler when the war began. He lived in Ilford with his parents and sister. His father was called up, but as he worked for a petrol company he was excused service. Mr Dudley was sent to the company depot at Bishop's Stortford in Hertfordshire and drove a tanker, delivering fuel to local airbases. The Dudley family moved to Bishop's Stortford, too. They lived close to Cecil Rhodes's house by the River Stort. There was an American army base nearby and Bill remembers asking the GIs for chewing gum, using the famous phrase, 'Got any gum, chum?' sometimes he was lucky, but not always.

Mr Dudley would often take Bill to the aircraft factory at Sawbridgeworth where Mosquitoes were made. They would collect off-cuts of balsa wood, which was used in production, and Mr Dudley made them into model aircraft as Christmas gifts for children in hospital. There was also a dump on the Newmarket road where Bill used to find parts of crashed aircraft.

Although he was not an evacuee, Bill always felt that he did not fit in with other children in the area because he was an outsider. The parents of local children would tell him to go away when he called at their houses to ask to play. The Dudley youngsters used to play in a bombed house that backed on to the American base and from the garden they could see into the camp. Bill remembers that unlike other camps where the soldiers put on parties for children and gave them sweets, at the end of the war the servicemen burnt huge piles of chocolate before leaving to go home. One of Bill's friends stole a large dummy bomb that used to hang on the fence outside the camp as a signpost. All the local children signed it and the boy kept it in his bedroom.

While there were still British prisoners in German camps, there were also many enemy soldiers held at sites throughout Essex. Ten of the German prisoners from Purfleet Camp were set to clear bomb damage in Park Lane, Romford. They were guarded by three military policemen carrying Sten guns. A Southend man was fined £5 at Brentwood for buying baskets from Italian prisoners of war. The charge against the man, who was the coach driver responsible for taking the Italians to work, was that he had prejudiced the discipline of POWs by giving them British money.

Sweets were in short supply during the war but the end of hostilities in Europe brought the promise that some would be back soon. (Mars and Maltesers are registered trade marks. Used with permission from Mars UK Limited)

The royal family acknowledge the crowds after victory is declared.

As the war drew to its end the public were shown cinema newsreels of the horrors committed in the death camps in Germany. It was the first evidence of what had been going on: audiences were shocked and in many cases moved to tears.

The *Essex County Standard* chose an unusual photograph for its front page to celebrate the end of the war. It did not show one of the street parties or the victorious return of conquering heroes. It pictured a warden standing outside his sandbagged hut in 1939. The *Standard* said the image demonstrated the spirit that had won the war. The warden did not know what was coming as he stood there that day, but he was ready to face whatever was thrown at him.

Victory in Europe Day, 7 May, was followed by a 'Victory Show' put on by the soldiers from Shoebury Garrison. The show was a thank you to locals for their support during the war. Weapons that had remained top secret during the conflict were put on display and for a shilling some could even be fired at targets out at sea. During the three-day show, daylight hours were taken up with fairs and displays by the soldiers, evenings with dances to music played by military bands. It was an enthusiastic return to fun and enjoyment after the austerity of the war years. It was also a forerunner of the VE parties that were to sweep the county.

Street parties had been a way to celebrate coronations in the recent past, and the end of the war in Europe was the perfect excuse for new outdoor celebrations. There was not a street without festoons and bunting – parties were quickly organised in every road.

In Romford a bonfire was built in Cottons Park. However, unable to wait for the official start to proceedings, someone lit the fire twenty-four hours early.

In Colchester bunting was put up everywhere. There were bonfires, fireworks and searchlight displays. However, many of the decorations were destroyed by hooligans and the Red Lion Hotel had to hire guards to protect its display. There were at least two examples in Colchester of released prisoners of war arriving home to their street while parties were going on. Although the war ended in 1945 celebrations went on into the following year in many parts of the county.

Jimmy Underwood from Dagenham missed VE Day after spending much of the war aboard HMS *Nigeria*. He had been hurt in an explosion and was in hospital in Portsmouth when the war ended. Although he wanted to stay in the navy after the war, he was discharged because of his wounds.

Peter Russell from Beauchamp Roding near Ongar remembers hearing about the end of the war on his radio. He spent VE Day riding his bike around Essex and calling in on local pubs to join in the celebrations. Sylvia Walker recalls that when her father came home to Dagenham from the army the neighbours put up flags and 'welcome home' signs on the walls of their houses. There were street parties everywhere.

The thoughts of many local councils now turned to housing, which was in short supply because of bomb damage. Many more homes were needed for returning military personnel and Hornchurch Council promised that ex-servicemen would be

Two schools unite for a victory party in Ilford. Note the Russian flag on the wall.

A victory party in Laburnum Walk, Hornchurch.

given preference over others on the waiting list. The council tried to obtain land close to Park Lane for new homes but the scheme met with objections from the Roneo company which owned the land and had planned to use it to build an extension to its factory.

Nevertheless, families left homeless by the bombing had to be rehoused. Small estates of prefabricated buildings began to appear all over the county. The government had planned to build half a million of these 'portal houses', named after Lord Portal, the Minister of Works and Planning.

The 'prefabs' were popular with their inhabitants – for many it was a first home of their own. In Barking, however, the local council complained to the Ministry of Health that the American-built prefabs were dangerous. Notices were put up on the walls warning residents not to bang in nails because of the risk of hitting an electric cable. In Dagenham there were complaints about the temporary housing erected, mainly on allotment sites. Councillor F. Grindrod likened the Nissen huts to large Anderson shelters.

Even the new estates of prefabs were not large enough to solve the housing shortage and several old army camps were taken over by squatters who had nowhere else to go. At first there were attempts to remove them, but some enterprising

FOOD FACTS

RE-REGISTER
for
MILK
with your present retailer

When you have your new ration book, you must re-register for milk, as well as for your rationed foods.

But there's a difference. If you want to, you can re-register with a new shop for your meat and your fats, and so on. But *you cannot change your milk retailer.* You must re-register with the one you are getting your milk from now. Why is the Ministry of Food asking you to do this? It's because so many people have changed their addresses that the records have become out of date, and that's bad for everyone — the Ministry, the retailers and you. The Ministry wants to make completely new records in order to be sure that the milk goes where it's needed.

So it's in your interests to re-register promptly. It's very easy.

THIS IS WHAT YOU MUST DO:

(1)   A special card will be given to you with your new ration book. Fill up this card as soon as possible and give it to your present milk retailer or his roundsman.

(2)   When you fill up page 6 of the ration book with the names and addresses of the shop where you intend to register for other foods, do not forget to include your *present* milk retailer.

RE-REGISTER AS SOON AS YOU GET YOUR NEW RATION BOOK

The war in Europe may have been over but rationing was not. This advertisement tells the public to re-register for milk rations.

councils decided to let them stay and pay rent. Some camps were still in use by the public until the mid-fifties.

In Colchester the waiting list numbered over 1,000 for 37 prefabs under construction. Building was slowed down by restrictive red tape and lack of skilled labour, and the waiting lists grew longer. There were also plans to build twenty-six temporary asbestos houses. (The dangers posed by the material were not known at the time.) The houses had a wooden frame and a felt roof. The council promised that it would use a reputable firm of builders and not prisoners of war to erect them.

An unusual event occurred in an Essex village at the end of the war. Residents of Tiptree campaigned to save an American soldier who was accused of attacking a villager. They spent two years petitioning the US authorities to get a court-martial decision overturned. Charles Schaffer was accused of assaulting a married woman after a dance in Tiptree in 1943. The inhabitants of the village had asked that new

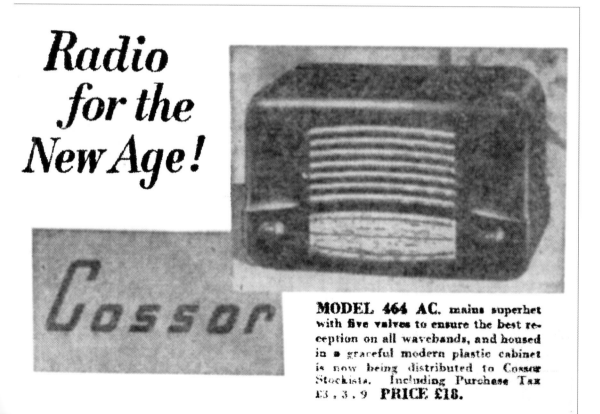

Radio for the New Age!

Cossor

MODEL 464 AC. mains superhet with five valves to ensure the best reception on all wavebands, and housed in a graceful modern plastic cabinet is now being distributed to Cossor Stockists. Including Purchase Tax £3.3.9 **PRICE £18.**

"FIRST IN THE WORLD TO PRODUCE RADAR RECEIVERS"

The end of the war brought a new age, a good selling tactic for a modern radio.

14 Reasons Why

THE MODERN ARMY OFFERS YOU A SPLENDID CAREER

Keen, eager, fit young men—here is news that vitally affects YOU! Conditions in Britain's regular army are being vastly improved—with rewards, status and prospects second to those of no other calling. Do YOU want a life with adventure, travel, comradeship—with training in skilled craftsmanship and progressive education? Do YOU want a job with security—fine pensions—good living conditions — regular sport — physical fitness? Then the modern regular army is the place for you. Study the panel on the right now. Then—

GET THIS FREE BOOK TO-DAY. Ask to-day, at any principal Post Office, Combined Recruiting Centre or Employment Exchange (or write to Dept. A.10, War Office, AG. 10, London, S.W.1) for *free* copy of " *The Army, the Modern Career* "—72 pages with many photographs, full details of pay, jobs, conditions of service, etc.

READ THESE POINTS

1 *Opportunity for every man to be a* SKILLED SPECIALIST; *a craft or trade to fit every aptitude. Valuable technical training free.* 2 *Good pay; no fares to work; no doctor's or clothing bills; good food and plenty of it.* 3 *Generous increased pensions for long service.* 4 *Security—no unemployment. Good prospects on return to "civvy street," skilled and fit.* 5 *Only 5 years' minimum colour service.* 6 *Better conditions and allowances for the married soldier.* 7 *Ample leisure time; plain clothes may be worn off duty.* 8 *Generous leave on full pay.* 9 *Free education in a vast number of subjects.* 10 *Plenty of sport and games; glorious physical fitness!* 11 *Training as a leader of men—self-confident and mentally alert.* 12 *Except for a very few, e.g. doctors, all officers graduate through the ranks. Merit now the sole test.* 13 *World travel (maximum overseas service 3½ years); adventure; lasting comradeship.* 14 *The* SATISFACTION AND PRIDE *of doing a fine job.*

EQUAL OPPORTUNITIES ! Nowadays every man is judged for advancement on his own merits.

The end of the war did not put an end to the demand for men for the army – note the boast of equal opportunities, a very modern idea for a postwar advertisement.

evidence be taken into account. When this did not happen, 300 petitioned the authorities. Schaffer was returned to duty. The vicar, Mr Hitchcock, said the villagers knew Schaffer was not guilty.

Although the attacks on Essex ended with the defeat of Germany, the fighting was not over for all the county's men. John Smith from Romford was crossing the Brahmaputra River on a raft, chasing the Japanese and eating hard biscuit and

Savings schemes did not end with the fighting as this savings badge shows.

John Smith (left) and a friend relax in Rangoon after chasing the Japanese out of Burma. The Shwedagon Pagoda is visible in the background. *(John Smith)*

Not everyone from Essex was celebrating VE Day. Leonard Walden from Dagenham had said goodbye to his parents and gone to join his ship, the aircraft carrier *Indefatigable*. *(Brian Walden)*

THE SHIP'S COMPANY

OF

H.M.S. "INDEFATIGABLE"

Request the pleasure of your Company

AT THEIR DANCE

to be held on Board

Wednesday, 16th January, 1946

DANCING
7.30 to 12.00

By kind permission of
Captain MacIntyre, C.B.E., D.S.O., R.N.

After the war in the Far East was finally over, *Indefatigable* sailed to Australia. The crew held a dance to mark their departure. It was well into 1946 before Leonard Walden was demobbed.

Leonard Walden with two shipmates, before leaving to fight the Japanese, aboard the aircraft carrier *Indefatigable*.

Seafire planes aboard *Indefatigable*. They were responsible for the last dogfight of the war in the Pacific, long after VE Day. *(Brian Walden)*

John Smith in Ceylon after the war. His injury was not a war wound but an ankle broken while playing football, no doubt a result of dreaming of returning home to Romford instead of concentrating on the game. *(John Smith)*

Celebrations went on well after the end of the conflict as this programme for a victory tattoo at Warley Barracks shows.

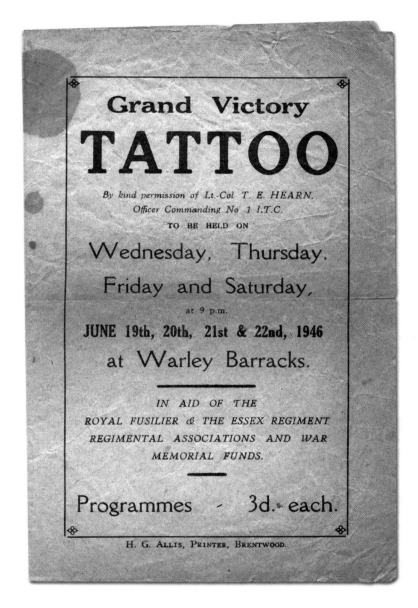

corned beef, when he heard on the field telephone that the war in Europe had ended. He learned that people in Britain were dancing in the streets and was pleased to know that his loved ones were now safe. John and his comrades were a little envious, however, not knowing how long they were going to be stuck in the 'hell hole' they found themselves in. The war ended for John a few months later but he did not get home until late in 1946.

In May 1945 Leonard Walden from Dagenham was a sailor aboard the aircraft carrier *Indefatigable*. The ship had been in the Far East fighting the Japanese and

was attacked by a kamikaze pilot in April. Seafire planes from the vessel were involved in the last dogfight of the war in August 1945.

Back home in Essex life began to get back to normal, or as normal as life can be after years of conflict. What had been commonplace before 1939 was not the norm now. The people of the county no longer lived their lives in small villages which they rarely left. Many had been to parts of the world they never knew existed before. Not only had people changed, so had the land, the buildings and the way of life.

There were huge VE Day celebrations in London in June 1946 and festivities also took place in parts of Essex. This is a Colchester Hippodrome Junior Club party. The Hippodrome had once been a theatre but was a cinema by this time.

Bibliography

BOOKS

Evans, Brian, *Romford, Collier Row & Gidea Park*, Phillimore, 1994

Everitt, Bryan, *The Story of Moore Brothers*, Bryan Everitt, 1998

Facts about British Railways in Wartime, British Railways Press Office, 1943

Invasion, 5th Essex Battalion Home Guard Booklet, 1941 (Essex Record Office)

Martin, Geoffrey, *Colchester, from Roman Times to the Present Day*, Benham, 1959

Penfold, John, *Essex County Hospital, Colchester*, Penfold, 1984

Richards, Glyn (ed.), *Ordeal in Romford*, Ian Henry Publications, 2005

Slinn, Judy, *A History of May & Baker*, Hobson, 1984

Thompson, R.J., *Battle Over Essex*, Essex War Welfare Committee, 1946

Trist, P., *Land Reclamation*, Faber & Faber, 1946

Williams, Samuel, *A Company's Story in its Setting*, Samuel Williams & Sons Ltd, 1955

Yearsley, Ian, *Essex Events*, Phillimore, 1999

NEWSPAPERS

Essex County Standard
Romford & Essex Times

Index